AN INVESTIGATION INTO USING NEWS ANALYTICS DATA IN GARCH TYPE VOLATILITY MODELS

Sergei P. Sidorov and Vladimir Balash

Sergei P. Sidorov (Saratov State University, Department of Mechanics and Mathematics, Saratov, Russian Federation)

Vladimir Balash (Saratov State University, Department of Mechanics and Mathematics, Saratov, Russian Federation)

AMS Subject Classification (2010): 91G70, 62P20, 91G30

© 2011 Sergei P. Sidorov, Vladimir Balash. All rights reserved.

ISBN 978-1-4709-2612-0 London Academic Press, United Kingdom

Printing and binding by LULU Publishing, USA

Contents

Abstract

In the work we study different dynamic volatility models. We consider the family of ARCH and GARCH models to compare the performance of the models using both unconditional coverage Kupiec's test and the test of conditional coverage proposed by Christoffersen. In-sample estimation procedure and out-of-sample evaluation will be based on General Electric stock market closing daily prices (January 2, 2008 - December 31, 2010).

We consider different volatility models augmented with news analytics data to examine the impact of news intensity on stock volatility. First we consider two types of GARCH models: augmented with volume and augmented with news intensity. Based on empirical evidences for some of FTSE100 companies it will be shown that the GARCH(1,1) model augmented with volume does remove GARCH and ARCH effects for the most of the companies, while the GARCH(1,1) model augmented with news intensity has difficulties in removing the impact of log return on volatility.

Then we compare GARCH model with jumps and GARCH–Jumps model augmented with news intensity using likelihood ratio test.

We also provide a description of the data used in the empirical analysis and defines the measures of news intensity. Results for the variance homogeneity tests for days with different news intensity are also given. We show that abnormal returns occur more likely in days with high news intensity.

We propose the different modifications of the SV model and suggest a way to test the hypothesis of a short-term impact of news intensity on volatility. The results show that news analytics data improves the quality of prediction of volatility of the SV model. For almost all FTSE100 companies, the hypothesis of a short-term impact of news on stock volatility is accepted. Negative news increase short-term stock volatility more likely than positive news.

The study shows that the problem of examining the impact of news intensity on volatility is far more sophisticated than it might seem at first sight. Some hypothesists and suggestions for future work are proposed in the final chapter.

Acknowledgements

Our profound thanks to Dr Paresh Date (Brunel University) and Keming Yu (Brunel University) for helpful discussions. In addition we would like to express my immense gratitude to Prof Gautam Mitra, Director of CARISMA, for creative support and for the kindly provided opportunity to use Raven Pack news analytics data.

This work could not have been written without financial support of Russian Government Programme "Innovative University" and organizational support of Tatyana Zakharova, pro-vice chancellor of Saratov State University, as well as the staff of managerial board of the programme "Innovative University".

Chapter 1

Introduction

The reactions of asset prices and market volatility to information concerning fundamental variables are of key interest for such financial and economic decisions as risk management, asset pricing, and portfolio allocation. Volatility analysis of financial time series is an important aspect of many financial decisions. For example, fund managers, option traders and etc., are all interested in volatility forecasts in order to either construct less risky portfolios or obtain higher profits. Hence, there is always a need for good analysis and forecasting of volatility.

In this work we focus on the stock volatility and some adequate models of its dynamics. GARCH models are used by many researchers and practitioners to generate volatility forecasts. GARCH models give useful and quite reliable estimates of the conditional stock variance. Since the appearance, the ARCH and GARCH models proved their effectiveness. It is known that one of advantages of the ARCH and GARCH models is simple parameterization.

On the other hand, this models cannot capture the asymmetric effect discovered by Black (1976). This effect occurs when an unexpected drop in price (bad news) increases predictable volatility more than an unexpected increase in price (good news) of similar magnitude. This effect suggests that a symmetry constraint on the conditional variance function in past is inappropriate. So we are going to apply some asymmetric models (including EGARCH, GJR-GARCH and Threshold GARCH). To validate the calibrated model we will use out-of-sample evaluation procedure.

Since GARCH model cannot explain observed changes in stock volatility, the question is what are the core factors driving its behavior. In our quest we will rely on the Mixture of Distribution Hypothesis (MDH). MDH suggests that the stock volatility is closely related to the information frequency. We are going to analyze the impact of news on stock volatility by considering tree types of models:

1. *Augmented GARCH models.* Augmented GARCH models allows us to indirectly test the Mixture of Distribution Hypothesis (MDH). We use two different proxy for the mixing variable

   - Following the study of Lamoureux and Lastrapes Lamoureax and Lastrapes [1990] we will suppose that trading volume can be considered as a proportional proxy for information arrivals to the market. We will show that once contemporaneous volume is included as an exogenous variable in the model, the GARCH persistence effect diminishes.
   - Kalev and al. (2004), Cousin and Launois [2006] considered the "daily number of press releases on a stock" (news intensity) as the most appropriate explanatory variable in the basic equation of GARCH model. Following their studies we will examine the GARCH model with news intensity using news analytics data from Raven Pack, one of the biggest providers of news analytics in the world.

2. *GARCH–Jumps Model augmented with news analytics data.*

3. *The stochastic volatility model.* We assume that conditional variance of returns depends on some hidden process that represents news arrival. To measure the effect of conditional variance of stock returns on the intensity of the news flow we investigate some probability distributions of stock returns. Innovations of the stock returns process are often considered to be the latent stochastic process that represents the impact of news on the stock returns. We postulate that a latent process has two separate components which account for regular news and unexpected news events. It is possible that regular news has smaller impact on returns and expected volatility for individual stocks that unexpected news events. It can be assumed that small volatility fluctuations are influenced by the regular news. Unexpected

news causes bigger jumps in returns, and, consequently, in volatility. A potential source of jump-like innovations in the return process could be news about important of events.

To calibrate this models we will use two types of input data: stock prices (source: Yahoo!Finance); news sentiment scores (source: RavenPack News Scores.

The work is organized as follows.

Chapter 2 provides a brief review of the literature about ARCH and GARCH models, the relation between information and conditional volatility.

Chapter 3 introduces notation and describes two methods of calibration of models: the maximum likelihood estimator and generalized moments method.

Chapter 4 presents a short introduction to volatility measurement.

Chapter 6 is a short review of the tools, methods and providers of news analytics and mostly based on the book Mitra and Mitra [2011]. The chapter also provides a description of the data used in the empirical analysis and defines the measures of news intensity. Results for the variance homogeneity tests for days with different news intensity are also given. We also show that abnormal returns occur more likely in days with high news intensity.

In Chapter 5 one can find description of the family of ARCH and GARCH models. Asymmetric GARCH models also are presented. Empirical study consists of in-sample estimation and out-of-sample forecast evaluation of VaR to estimate predictive properties of the models.

Chapter 7 of the work presents augmented GARCH models. Empirical results are obtained based on two different data sets: stock prices and Raven Pack news wires.

Chapter 8 presents two different GARCH models with jumps. We will consider the problem of calibration of the models and give some empirical results.

Chapter 9 presents a review of the literature regarding the stochastic volatility model. Chapter 10 reports estimation results for different SV models.

Chapter 11 concludes and provides some perspectives for future research.

Chapter 2

Literature Review

It is well-known that financial data are usually serial dependent. Moreover, distribution of the data is often heavy-tailed, asymmetric and therefore not Gaussian and volatility changes over time. The ARCH model was introduced by R. Engle (Engle [1982]). The model describes quite well the stylized facts of financial data and is also relatively simple and stationary. R. Engle called his model autoregressive conditionally heteroskedastic – ARCH, because the conditional variance (squared volatility) is not constant over time and shows autoregressive structure. This model is a convenient way of modelling time-dependent conditional variance. Some years later, Bollerslev [1986] generalized this model as the GARCH model (Generalized Autoregressive Conditional Heteroscedasticity).

Since the appearance, the ARCH and GARCH models proved their effectiveness. It is clear that one of advantages of the ARCH and GARCH models is simple parametrization. On the other hand, this models cannot capture the asymmetric effect discovered by Black in the paper Black [1976]. This feature was also confirmed by Kenneth R. French, G. William Schwert and Robert F. Stambaugh French et al. [1987], D. Nelson Nelson [1990], and G. William Schwert Schwert [1990], among others.

This effect occurs when an unexpected drop in price (bad news) increases predictable volatility more than an unexpected increase in price (good news) of similar magnitude. This effect suggests that a symmetry constraint on the conditional variance function in past innovations is inappropriate.

To capture the asymmetric effects a few models were introduced. The most commonly used asymmetric GARCH models are:

1. Exponential GARCH (EGARCH) model (Nelson [1991]);

2. The Quadratic GARCH (QGARCH) model (Sentana [1995]);

3. The Glosten-Jagannathan-Runkle GARCH (GJR-GARCH) model (Glosten et al. [1993]);

4. The Threshold GARCH (TGARCH) model (Zakoian [1994]).

There are well-known empirical studies of the positive contemporaneous correlation between trading volume and price volatility. In the paper Karpoff [1987] one can find the review of previous research on the relation between price changes and trading volume in financial markets. It cites about 20 papers that examine this relation in financial markets including equities, futures, currencies, and Treasury bills. Some of these papers also document an asymmetry in the relation; positive price shocks are associated with larger volumes than are negative price shocks.

Trading volume is one of the most favored proxies for news arrivals. It can be explained by the following way: the more specific news arrives about a given stock (or company), the more investors will interpret the effects of that news differently, and thus the more investors will have an incentive to trade as their expectations about future returns diverge. There are several theoretical models have been proposed to explain this relationship, for example, "asymmetric information" model, "differences in opinion" model, the sequential information arrival hypothesis, and the "mixture of distributions" model.

Mixture of Distribution Hypothesis (MDH) was proposed for the first time by Clark (Clark [1973]). It assumes that the joint distribution of daily return and volume can be modeled as a mixture of multivariate normal distributions. The main idea of MDH is that returns on financial assets are generated from a mixture of distributions in which the stochastic mixture variable is considered to be the rate of arrival of information flow into the market. Specifically, they are contemporaneously dependent on an underlying mixing variable that represents the flow of information. As a consequence, the variance of returns at a given interval is expected to be proportional to the rate of information arrival at the market. The development of MDH can be found in the papers Epps and Epps [1976], and Tauchen and Pitts [1983].

The paper Lamoureax and Lastrapes [1990] examine the validity of MDH for daily stock returns. It exploits the implication of the MDH that the volatility of daily price increments is positively related to the rate of daily information arrival. They suggest the daily trading volume as a measure of the amount of information flowing into the market every day. The authors used daily trading volume as a proxy for mixing variable and showed that ARCH and GARCH coefficients vanish if volume is included as an explanatory variable in the GARCH model.

Lamoureux and Lastrapes (Lamoureax and Lastrapes [1990]) used daily trading volume as a proxy for the mixing variable. They showed that the introduction of volume as an exogenous variable in the conditional variance equation eliminates the persistence of GARCH effects as measured by the sum of the GARCH parameters.

After the work of Lamoureax and Lastrapes [1990], a number of papers studying this issue have been appeared. However, the findings are not consistent. For example, the paper Sharma et al. [1996] tests for the Generalized Autoregressive Conditional Heteroscedasticity (GARCH) effects in stock market indicator returns using the NYSE daily return and volume data for four years. The study shows that the market indicator returns are best described by the simple GARCH model (without volume as a mixing variable). Moreover, it was shown that the inclusion of volume as a proxy for information arrival in the conditional variance model does not necessary lead to the decrease of the GARCH effects.

In the paper Arago and Nieto [2005] investigate the issue for market index data for nine countries. It was found that volume effects do not cancel out GARCH effects at the country index level. In the paper Arago and Nieto [2005] unexpected trading volume uses as a proxy variable for the information flow. It was shown that the inclusion of trading volume does not reduce the persistence of conditional volatility.

On the other hand, there are some papers with findings analogous to Lamoureax and Lastrapes [1990]. For example, Pagunathan and Peker Ragunathan and Peker [1997] a strong contemporaneous effect of trading volume on volatility in the Sydney Futures Exchange. In the paper Miyakoshi [2002] one can find that the inclusion of the trading volume variable in EGARCH models eliminates the ARCH/-GARCH effect for individual stocks as well as for the index on the Tokyo Stock Exchange. Bohl and Henke (2003) examine Polish stock markets and obtain similar results.

The paper Xiao et al. [2009] examines the quantitative relationship between volume and volatility in the Australian Stock Market. The authors study interaction of GARCH and volume effects on the entire available data for the Australian All Ordinaries Index. They showed that GARCH model testing and estimation is impacted by trading volume. In the paper the daily trading volume was used as a proxy for information arrival time. It is shown that the daily trading volume have significant explanatory power regarding the variance of daily returns. They also studied the impact of firm size on volatility. It was shown that the actively traded stocks with larger number of information arrivals per day have a larger impact of volume on the variance of daily returns, while low trading volume and small firm lead to a higher persistence of GARCH effects in the estimated models.

Thus, it is still interesting to investigate this issue with a new proxy variable for the information flow. One of them might be the news intensity (the number of news about a company at the day t is called the news intensity at the day t). There are not so much studies tried to examine relation between flows of information and stock (or market) volatility. One of the reason for that is the difficulty to find good empirical proxy of information arrivals.

Different measures of information arrivals were employed in variety of empirical studies in order to test the impact of the rate of information on the market volatility:

- macroeconomic news, Ederington and Lee [1993];

- the number of daily newspaper headlines and earnings announcements, Berry and Howe [1993];

- the number of specific stock market announcements, Mitchell and Mulherin

[1994].

It was written in the paper Kalev et al. [2004] that "the use of unconditional volatility measures such as absolute daily market returns in these studies often generates weak or inconclusive results regarding the news-volatility relation". Indeed, a news intensity is known to be quite noisy, and the presence of conditional heteroscedasticity in the returns time-series may significantly destroys the quality of the results.

It is worth mentioning the paper Andersen [1996] in which it was shown that different types of news have a different impact on the conditional stock volatility.

In the paper of Kalev et al. [2004] it was used firm-specific announcements as a proxy for information flows. It was shown that there exists a positive and significant impact of the arrival rate of the selected news variable on the conditional variance of stock returns on the Australian Stock Exchange in a GARCH framework. They split all their press releases into different categories according to their subject.

Some authors have worked specifically on the French market (Cousin and Launois [2006]).

Chapter 3

Preliminaries

3.1 Notation

Let X be a random variable defined on a probability space (Ω, Σ, P). Let F be the cumulative distribution function of X:

$$F(x) := P(X \leq x).$$

The mean of the random variable X (or the expected value of X) can be defined as

$$\mu = \mathbb{E}(X) = \int_{\mathbb{R}} x \, dF(x). \tag{3.1}$$

If the integral (3.1) exists, i.e. the random variable X has the mean μ, then the variance of X is defined by

$$\sigma^2 = Var(X) = \mathbb{E}((X - \mu)^2), \tag{3.2}$$

the variance is defined as the average squared deviation of each number from its mean.

Standard deviation of X is the square of the variance:

$$\sigma = \sqrt{Var(X)}.$$

The variance measures how spread out a distribution is. The variance is the one of the most used volatility measures.

Variance has the following properties.

1. Variance of a random X is equal to 0 if and only if X is a constant random variable.

2. Let $a \in \mathbb{R}$, X be a random variable, then

$$Var(aX) = a^2 Var(X).$$

3. Let $b \in \mathbb{R}$, X be a random variable, then

$$Var(X + b) = Var(X).$$

4. Let X, Y be random variables with cumulative distribution functions F_X and F_Y respectively, then

$$Var(X + Y) = Var(X) + Var(y) + 2Cov(X, Y),$$

where

$$Cov(X, Y) = \int \int xy dF_X(x) dF_Y(y).$$

Note that $Cov(X, X)$ is just $Var(X)$.

5. Let X be a random variable with $|\mathbb{E}(X)| < \infty$, then

$$Var(X) = \mathbb{E}(X^2) - (\mathbb{E}(X))^2.$$

6. Let X, Y be random variables with $|\mathbb{E}(X)| < \infty$ and $|\mathbb{E}(Y)| < \infty$, then

$$Var(XY) = (\mathbb{E}(X))^2 Var(Y) + (\mathbb{E}(Y))^2 Var(X) + Var(X) Var(Y).$$

Consider the case when X is a discrete random variable. Let $x_1, \ldots, x_N$ be a population of the length N. Then the population mean is defined as

$$\mu = \frac{1}{N} \sum_{i=1}^{N} x_i.$$

The population variance is defined by

$$\sigma^2 = \frac{1}{N} \sum_{i=1}^{N} (x_i - \mu)^2.$$

When we are dealing with some empirical data, it is difficult or impossible to know exactly distribution of random variable X. So we can not apply (3.1) to find the value of the variance of X. Then usually the variance is estimated based on a sample.

Let $y_1, \ldots, y_n$ be a sample (i.e. finite number of realizations of a discrete or continuous random variable X). Then the sample mean

$$\bar{y} = \frac{1}{n} \sum_{i=1}^{n} y_i$$

is estimator of the mean of the random variable X.

To estimate the variance $Var(X)$ of the random variable X we can use two estimators.

1. The variance of the sample

$$s_n^2 = \frac{1}{n} \sum_{i=1}^{n} (y_i - \bar{y})^2.$$

   Note that $\mathbb{E}(s_n^2) = \frac{n-1}{n}\sigma^2$.

2. The unbiased estimator of the variance

$$s^2 = \frac{1}{n-1} \sum_{i=1}^{n} (y_i - \bar{y})^2.$$

Unbiased means that $\mathbb{E}(s^2) = \sigma^2$, i.e. the expected value of the sample estimator coincides with the theoretical value of the variance.

Consider a random variable X distributed normally with mean μ and variance σ^2, $X \sim \mathcal{N}(\mu, \sigma^2)$. About 68% of values drawn from a normal distribution are within one standard deviation s away from the mean; about 95% of the values lie within two standard deviations; and about 99.7% are within three standard deviations. This fact is known as the 68-95-99.7 rule, or the empirical rule, or the 3-sigma rule. To be more precise, the probability of that X lies between $\mu - n\sigma$ and $\mu + n\sigma$ is given by

$$P(\mu - n\sigma \leq X \leq \mu + n\sigma) = \Phi(n) - \Phi(-n), \tag{3.3}$$

where

$$\Phi(x) := \frac{1}{\sqrt{2\pi}} \int_{-\infty}^{x} \exp^{-t^2/2} dt.$$

3.2   Calibration of models

3.2.1   The maximum likelihood estimator

In this subsection we will shortly describe this method as well as its shortcomings and advantages. We can refer the reader to the paper Le Cam [1990] for a deep study and a related bibliography.

We will use maximum likelihood for calibration the GARCH model in Chapter 5.

Let

$$x_1, x_2, \ldots, x_n \tag{3.4}$$

be an vector of observations of length n. We suppose that x_i are realizations of a random variable ζ with an unknown distribution density f. It is assumed that the density $f(\cdot)$ belongs to a parameterized family of distributions

$$\mathcal{F} := \{ f(\cdot | \theta) : \theta \in \Theta \}.$$

Denote θ^* the vector of the true values of parameters. We need to find θ^0 so that θ^0 would be close to θ^* as much as possible in some sense.

The joint density function for observation sequence (3.4) is

$$f(x_1, \ldots, x_n | \theta) = f(x_1 | \theta) \cdot f(x_2 | \theta) \cdot \ldots \cdot f(x_n | \theta) = \prod_{t=1}^{n} f(x_t | \theta).$$

Let us to view the likelihood function as a probability density for θ, and to think of $f(x_1, \ldots, x_n | \theta)$ as the conditional density of θ given $x_1, \ldots, x_n$:

$$L(\theta | x_1, \ldots, x_n) = f(x_1, \ldots, x_n | \theta).$$

The function $L(\theta | x_1, \ldots, x_n)$ is called *the likelihood function*.

We need to find $\theta^0 \in \Theta$ that maximizes the likelihood function $L(\theta | x_1, \ldots, x_n)$ over all $\theta \in \Theta$, given $x_1, \ldots, x_n$. In many cases it is much easy to maximize the logarithm value of the function:

$$\log L(\theta | x_1, \ldots, x_n) = \sum_{t=1}^{n} \log f(x_t | \theta). \tag{3.5}$$

The function (3.5) is called *the log-likelihood function*.

There are many models in which a maximum likelihood estimator can be found as an explicit function of the observed data $x_1, \ldots, x_n$, i.e. in Gaussian case.

However, for the most models there is not closed-form solution to the maximization problem

$$\log L(\theta | x_1, \ldots, x_n) \rightarrow \max_{\theta \in \Theta}, \tag{3.6}$$

and a maximum likelihood estimation has to be found numerically using optimization methods.

The maximum likelihood estimator θ^0 is defined by

$$\theta^0 = \arg \max_{\theta \in \Theta} \log L(\theta | x_1, \ldots, x_n).$$

Thus we are choosing θ to maximize the probability of occurrence of the observation $x_1, \ldots, x_n$.

We point out some attractive asymptotic properties of the maximum-likelihood estimator:

1. **Consistency:** the maximum likelihood estimator θ^0 converges in probability to the value θ^* being estimated, i.e. $\theta^0 \to \theta^*$ as the number of observations n tends to ∞.

2. **Asymptotic normality:** as the sample size increases, the distribution of the MLE tends to the Gaussian distribution with mean θ and covariance matrix equal to the inverse of the Fisher information matrix. (see e.g. Myung and Navarro [2005]).

3. **Efficiency**, i.e., it achieves the Cramér–Rao lower bound when the sample size tends to infinity. This means that no asymptotically unbiased estimator has lower asymptotic mean squared error than the MLE.

It is worth noting that problem (3.6) is often non-convex and, thus, finding its exact solution is in principle a difficult task. Optimization methods may include gradient climbing algorithms such as Newton-Raphson and EM algorithm.

Moreover, local minima are indeed a problem: different initial sets of parameters yield a different local minimum. But the problem is not only multiple local minima, also that quite often solutions are in the boundary of the feasible parameter space, e.g. some variances of the noises are estimated to have value zero. We will encounter this problem in Chapter 8.

3.2.2   Generalized moments method

Sometimes we do not know the shape of the distribution function of the data, but we can assume which of parameterized set of functions our distribution belongs to. In such cases the maximum likelihood estimation can not be apply, but the generalized moment method can be useful.

Let $y_1, y_2, \ldots, y_n$ be a sample from a distribution governed by parameter θ. A function $e(y)$ is said to be *sample statistic* if it is a function of sample observations $y_1, y_2, \ldots, y_n$ alone.

We say that an estimator $e(y)$ is *unbiased* if $\mathbb{E}(e(y)) = \theta$. If $\mathbb{E}(e(y)) \neq \theta$ then the value $\mathbb{E}(e(y)) - \theta$ is the bias of the estimator $e(y)$.

An estimator $e(y)$ is said to be *minimum variance unbiased* if it is unbiased and for every any other unbiased estimator e^* of θ we have $\text{Var}(e(y)) \leq \text{Var}(e^*(y))$.

We say that an estimator $e(y)$ is consistent if $e(y)$ converges to θ in probability as $n \to \infty$.

First we consider classical moment methods. Classical moment methods is a simple method for estimating unknown parameters in different statistical models.

Let $\theta \in \mathbb{R}^m$ be a vector of parameters (moments) that characterize the distribution of random variable y. Let the distribution function of the random variable y belongs to parameterized family of distributions $\{F(\cdot, \theta) : \theta \in \Theta\}$. The k-th moment (if it exists) of distribution of random variable y is defined as

$$m_k(\theta) = \mathbb{E}(y^k) = \int_{\mathbb{R}} y^k dF(y, \theta). \tag{3.7}$$

If we have sample observations $y_1, y_2, \ldots, y_n$ (considered as n independent random variables), then we can find k-th sample moment as follows

$$\hat{m}_k = \frac{1}{n} \sum_{i=1}^{n} y_i^k \tag{3.8}$$

Suppose we know the values some of the moments $\hat{m}_k$, $k \in I$, where $I \subset \mathbb{N}$, $|I| = k$. The main idea of method of moments is to estimate unknown parameters θ by matching "theoretical" moments (3.7) and sample moments (3.8) of the same orders:

$$m_k(\theta) = \hat{m}_k, \ k \in I. \tag{3.9}$$

In general, method of moments estimators are consistent whenever the Law of Large Numbers ensures that the sample moments in the data-generating process converge in probability to the corresponding population moments.

The classical method of moments can be applied if $m = k := |I|$. It follows from the fact that the number of unknown parameters is equal to the number of equations in (3.9) that the system (3.9) has a solution. If $m < k$ then (3.9) does not have a solution.

The first idea is to exclude $k - m$ equations and then apply the classical method of moments. The question is which of equations must be discard? The generalized method of moments technique uses all k moment conditions by weighting them, i.e. it chooses an estimator that balances each moment condition against the others. A GMM estimator may satisfy no one moment condition, but it may come close to satisfying them all.

Let data be a finite number of realizations of the process x_t, $t = 1, 2, \ldots, N$. Let the model is satisfied a vector of moment conditions:

$$\mathbb{E}(f(x_t, \theta^*)) = 0 \qquad (3.10)$$

where $x_t \in \mathbb{R}^r$ is an vector of observable variables, $\theta^* \in \mathbb{R}^m$ is a vector of true value of parameters and $f : \mathbb{R}^r \times \mathbb{R}^m \to \mathbb{R}^k$ is a vector valued function. We assume that on the parameter space $\mathbb{E}(f(x_t, \theta)) = 0$ if and only if $\theta = \theta^*$.

Sample analogue of (3.10) can be written as

$$g_N(\theta) = \frac{1}{N} \sum_{t=1}^{N} f(x_t, \theta).$$

Suppose that we have a sequence of $k \times k$ positive semi definite matrix W_N converging to a positive definite matrix W_0. Then, GMM estimator is defined as

$$\hat{\theta} = \arg \inf_{\theta} (g_N'(\theta) W_N g_N(\theta)).$$

GMM does not guarantee an efficient estimator, but it does provide a consistent estimator, and its weighting scheme is more efficient than the simpler unweighted scheme Ravi et al. [2002].

We refer readers to the paper Hall [2004] for more details.

Chapter 4

Volatility

4.1 What is volatility

Volatility can be described as the relative rate at which the price of a security moves up and down. Volatility may be found by calculating the annualized standard deviation of daily change in price. Usually volatility describes the behavior of a financial instrument for a specified period of time, i.e. 1 day or 30 days or 90 days.

The measurement of the volatility of a financial instrument may be based on historical prices over the specified period. In this case it is obvious that the last observations the most recent price are needed to get more precise prediction of this behavior. It is supposed that if the price of a stock moves up and down rapidly over short time periods, then it has high volatility. And vice-versa: if the price has small changes or almost never changes, it has low volatility.

It is worth noting that there are different types of volatility:

- *the actual current volatility* of an instrument,

- *actual historical volatility* which refers to the volatility of a financial instrument over a specified period with dates in the past,

- *actual future volatility* which refers to the volatility of a financial instrument over a specified period starting at the current time and ending at a future date (normally the expiry date of an option),

- *historical implied volatility*, i.e. the volatility of the price of the underlying security. It is implied by the market price of the option based on an option pricing model,

- *current implied volatility* which refers to the implied volatility observed from current prices of the financial instrument,

- *future implied volatility* which refers to the implied volatility observed from future prices of the financial instrument

If we consider the problem option pricing then there are several variables that are of interest in financial engineering. They include

- the current asset price,

- the strike price,

- time to maturity,

- the risk free rate,

- volatility.

The first four of them are known. Their values can be directly obtained or derived from current market data. The volatility of a stock is the only variable that can not be so easily found.

4.2   Volatility measurement

4.2.1   Variance

It is supposed that volatility is a measure of the range (dispersion) of an asset price about its mean value over a certain amount of time. Then it follows that volatility is connected to the variance of an asset price. A stock is said to be volatile if the price will vary greatly over time. Conversely, a less volatile stock will have a price that will deviate relatively little over time.

The variance measures how spread out a distribution is. The variance is the one of the most used volatility measures.

4.2.2 Heteroscedasticity

A sequence of random variables is said to be heteroscedastic, if the random variables have different variances. Heteroskedasticity is one of the most important concept in finance. It is connected with the fact that market returns of an individual stock or index returns, returns of commodity and energy markets almost always exhibit heteroskedasticity.

Heteroskedasticity can be one of two following forms:

- A process is said to be *unconditionally heteroscedastic* if unconditional variances are not constant. It is known that stock or bond returns demonstrate heteroscedastic behavior. The prices exhibit non-constant volatility, but periods of low or high volatility are generally not known in advance.

- A process is said to be *conditionally heteroscedastic* if conditional variances are not constant. Oil prices exhibit unconditional heteroscedasticity. The prices tend to have higher volatilities during the Summer than during other seasons.

If a process is unconditionally heteroscedastic, then it is necessarily conditionally heteroscedastic. The converse is not true. If a process is not unconditionally heteroscedastic or not conditionally heteroscedastic, it is said to be unconditionally homoscedastic or conditionally homoscedastic, respectively.

In finance, a variety of models are used for conditionally heteroscedastic processes. These include

- autoregressive conditional heteroscedastic (ARCH) models;

- generalized ARCH (GARCH) models

- regime-switching models; and

- stochastic volatility models.

White test White [1980] is one of well-known methods to test for the presence of heteroscedasticity.

One can use also Engle Test for Conditional Heteroscedasticity (see e.g. Tsay [2005]).

4.2.3   Stock beta

One of the most important measure of volatility is a stock's beta. The popularity of stock beta is connected with the fact that its values are easy to interpret. For example, if the beta value of a particular stock is greater than 1, then the price of the stock has movements that are greater than the whole stock market. And vice-versa, if the beta value is less than 1, then the stock's price movements are less than those of the market. Investors can use a stock's beta to measure the risk of a security versus the market. A Beta of 1 value means the stock market is moving in the same direction as the Market Index.

The stock beta β_A of an individual stock A is a coefficient that describes the relationship between the movements of an individual stock versus the market itself. The stock beta of A can be found as follows [Levinson, Mark (2006). Guide to Financial Markets. London: The Economist (Profile Books). pp. 145ñ6. ISBN 1-86197-956-8.]

$$\beta_A = \frac{Cov(r_A, r_m)}{Var(r_m)}, \tag{4.1}$$

where

- r_A is the rate of return of asset A.

- r_m is the expected market return, i.e. the return the investor expects to receive from a stock market index such as the S&P 500. For example, over the last 17 years or so, the S&P 500 has yielded investors an average annual return of around 8.10

To calculate a stock's beta using (4.1) one needs the following sets of historical data (these returns can be daily, weekly or any period.):

- returns of the stock (or closing stock prices of the stock);

- returns of the index (or closing prices for the index that is chosen as a proxy for the stock market).

Based on this data, one can also use standard formula of linear regression. Then the slope of the fitted line from the linear least-squares calculation is the estimated β_A.

Stock beta values are a key element in using the well-known capital asset pricing model (CAPM).

Denote r the expected rate of return of a particular stock. Then we can calculate the expected rate of return on an investment as follows

$$r = r_f + \beta(r_m - r_f), \tag{4.2}$$

where r_f is the risk-free interest rate, i.e. the interest rate that the investor expects to receive from a risk-free investment. U.S. Treasury Bills or German Government bills may be considered as risk-free investment for US dollars or Euro respectively.

The equation (4.2) says that the expected return on an investment is equal to the return on a risk-free investment plus the risk premium that is associated with the stock market itself, adjusted for the relative risk of the common stock we have chosen.

Beta information may be a powerful tool when used appropriately. However, it may be misleading as well, since the calculations on which it is based are extracted from historical data. As a result no one can tell for sure what the value of beta will be the next year.

So, you can use beta in the short-term for the measurement of the risk of a particular stock's prices and their fluctuations. Beta is also useful in giving us an insight in the reaction of a stock to different changes in the market and interest rates.

Some critics of beta can be found in Klarman [1991]. It includes

- Beta looks backward and history is not always an accurate predictor of the future. Beta is calculated based on historical price movements, which may have little to do with how a company's stock is poised to move in the future. Because the measure relies on historical prices, it's not even possible to accurately calculate the beta of newly issued stocks.

- Beta suggests a stockís price volatility relative to the whole market, but that volatility can be upward as well as downward movement. In a sustained advancing market, a stock that is outperforming the whole market would have a beta greater than 1.

4.3   Risk estimation

4.3.1   Risk measures

Risk measures:

1. Value-at-Risk;

2. Tail conditional expectation;

3. Expected shortfall;

4. Entropic risk measure;

5. Superhedging price.

One of the most well-known risk measures is Value-at-Risk.

Given $\alpha \in (0, 1]$, the real number q is said to be α-*quantile* of the random variable X under the probability distribution P if one of the three properties is satisfied:

1. $P(X \leq q) \geq \alpha \geq 1 - P(X \leq q)$;

2. $P(X \leq q) \geq \alpha$ and $P(x \geq q) \geq 1 - \alpha$;

3. $F_X(q) \geq \alpha$ and $F_X(q^-) \leq \alpha$, where F_X is the cumulative distribution function of X, and $F_X(q^-) = \lim_{X \to q, \, X < q} F(x)$.

Jorion (Jorion [2001]) defines Value-at-Risk of an asset as "the quantile of the projected distribution of gains and losses over the target horizon. If α is selected confidence level, VaR corresponds to the $1 - \alpha$ lower-tail level":

Definition 1 *Given $\alpha \in (0, 1]$, we define the Value-at-Risk (VaR) at level α of the random X with distribution P as negative of the quantile q_α^+ of X, i.e.*

$$VaR_\alpha(X) = -\inf\{x : \ P(X \leq x) \geq \alpha\}.$$

For instance, with 95% confidence level, VaR should be such that it exceeds 5% of the total number of observations in the distribution.

The value-at-risk or VaR of a portfolio is defined to be the (dollar) loss that is expected to be exceeded only $\alpha \cdot 100\%$ of the time over a fixed time interval. If, for example, a financial institution reports a 1% VaR of \$ 10,000,000 over a 1 day horizon then this means that 1% of the time the institution would be expected to realize a loss in excess of \$10,000,000. The current regulatory framework requires that financial institutions use their own internal risk models to calculate and report their 1% value-at-risk, VaR (0.01), over a 10 day horizon.

Even though VaR is one of the most commonly used risk measures, it does not satisfy certain properties which are considered to be desirable in any risk measure. These properties are described next.

4.3.2   Properties of coherent risk measures

Denote $\Omega_t = \{\omega\}$ the set of all states of the world at the moment t. We suppose that all elements of the set Ω at the end of period t is known, but the probabilities of states are unknown.

Let X denotes the final worth (at the moment t) of a position for each element $\omega \in \Omega_t$. X is a random variable. Denote G the set of all risks, i.e. the set of all real-valued functions defined on Ω.

It is supposed that any mapping $\rho : G \to \mathbb{R}$ defined on G with range in $\mathbb{R}$ is *a measure of risk*.

A risk measure satisfying the following properties is called *coherent*.

Axiom 1 *(Monotonicity) For all $X, Y \in G$ such that $X \leq Y$, we have*

$$\rho(X) \geq \rho(Y).$$

Axiom 2 *(Positive homogeneity) For all $\alpha \geq 0$ and all $X \in G$, we have*

$$\rho(\alpha X) = \alpha \rho(X).$$

Axiom 3 *(Subadditivity) For all $X, Y \in G$, we have*

$$\rho(X + Y) \leq \rho(X) + \rho(Y).$$

The property 3 is based on the principle of diversification that states that the risk of portfolio always less or equal to risk of it parts.

Axiom 4 *(Translation invariance) For all $X \in G$ and all $\alpha \in \mathbb{R}$, we have*

$$\rho(X + \alpha) = \rho(X) - \alpha.$$

In particular, if $\alpha = \rho(X)$ then $\rho(X + \rho(X)) = 0$ for every $X \in G$. The property 4 states that adding cash amount to the initial position, one decreasing the risk measure on the same value.

VaR does not satisfy the sub-additivity property and therefore is not coherent risk measure.

In the next subsection, we look at the most common method of computing the Value at Risk.

4.3.3   Variance-Covariance Method

This approach is based on the assumption that the underlying market factors have a (multivariate) normal distribution. Then, under some additional assumptions, it is possible to find the distribution of assets (or portfolio) profits and losses. The distribution will be normal as well. Then we can use standard properties of the normal distribution (see (3.3)) to find the loss that equals or exceeds α percent of the time, i.e. $VaR(\alpha)$.

If a probability of $\alpha\%$ is used to find 1-day VaR, then VaR is equal to $f(\alpha)$ times the standard deviation of changes in portfolio value:

$$VaR_t(\alpha) = M_{t-1}f(\alpha)\sigma_t,$$

where M_{t-1} is amount of money invested at the moment $t-1$, $f(\alpha)$ is defined in Table 4.1, and σ_t is estimated volatility (standard deviation) at the moment t.

Table 4.1: The values of the multiplication factor at the formula for VaR estimation for different confidence levels

α	0.5%	1%	2.5%	5%	10%	25%
$f(\alpha)$	2.5758	2.3263	1.9600	1.6449	1.2816	0.6745

4.3.4   Capital Requirements for Market Risk

Despite that VaR models have some shortcomings, they have been accepted by banking regulators as a tools for calculating capital requirements for market risk. The current regulatory framework was set up in the 1988 Basle Capital Adequacy Accord. The document presents minimum capital requirements for banks' credit risk exposure.

In 1996 American bank regulatory agency release a settlement to the Accord. One of the approach proposed in the settlement (known as "internal models") is based on the Value-at-Risk estimates calculated on the basis of bank's internal risk measurement model using VaR at level 0.01 with 10-day horizon.

According to the settlement, a bank's market risk capital requirement at day t, MRC_t, has to be

$$ MRC_t = S_t \max \left\{ \frac{1}{60} \sum_{i=1}^{60} VaR_{t-i}(10,1), VaR_t(10,1) \right\} + SR_t, $$

where

- $VaR_i(10,1)$ denotes VaR at level 0.01 with 10-day horizon at the day i,

- S_t is a regulatory multiplication factor, which depends on the accuracy of bank's VaR model. It calculates based on the number of times that daily trading losses exceed the corresponding bank's VaR estimates over the last 250 trading days (see Table 4.2).

- SR_t is an additional capital charge.

Table 4.2: The values of the regulatory multiplication factor

Number of Exceptions (Out of 250 Trading Day	0-4	5	6	7	8	9	10 and more
Scaling Factor, S_t	3.00	3.40	3.50	3.65	3.75	3.85	4

Chapter 5

The Family of ARCH and GARCH models

5.1 Introduction

It is well-known that financial markets and investors react nervously to important news, economic crises, wars, political disorders or natural disasters. In such periods prices of financial assets may fluctuate very much. It means that the conditional variance for the given past

$$Var(X_t|I_{t-1}) := Var(X_t|X_{t-1}, X_{t-2}, \ldots)$$

is not constant over time and the process X_t is conditionally heteroscedastic. In the other words, volatility

$$\sigma_t = \sqrt{Var(X_t|I_{t-1})}$$

changes over time. Understanding the nature of such time dependence is very important for many macroeconomic and financial applications, e.g. irreversible investments, option pricing, asset pricing etc. Models of conditional heteroscedasticity for time series have a very important role in todayís financial risk management and its attempts to make financial decisions on the basis of the observed price asset data P_t in discrete time. Prices P_t are believed to be non-stationary so they are usually transformed in the so-called log–returns

$$X_t = \log P_t - \log P_{t-1}$$

Log returns are supposed to be stationary, at least in periods of time that are not too long. Very often in the past it was suggested that (X_t) represents a sequence of independent identically distributed random variable, in other words, that prices evolve like a random walk. Samuelson suggested modeling speculative prices in the continuous time with the geometric Brownian motion. Discretization of that model leads to a random walk with independent identically distributed Gaussian increments of log return prices in discrete time. This hypothesis was rejected in the early sixties. Empirical studies based on the log return time series data of some US stocks showed the following observations, the so-called stylized facts of financial data:

1. serial dependence are present in the data;

2. volatility changes over time;

3. distribution of the data is heavy-tailed, asymmetric and therefore not Gaussian.

These observations clearly show that a random walk with Gaussian increments is not a very realistic model for financial data. It took some time before R. Engle found a discrete model that described very well the previously mentioned stylized facts of financial data, but it was also relatively simple and stationary so the inference was possible. The ARCH model was introduced by Engle [1982]. Engle called his model autoregressive conditionally heteroscedastic – ARCH, because the conditional variance (squared volatility) is not constant over time and shows autoregressive structure. This model is a convenient way of modeling time-dependent conditional variance. Some years later, Bollerslev [1986] generalized this model as the GARCH model (Generalized Autoregressive Conditional Heteroscedasticity).

5.2   ARCH Model

The primary idea is to use the rolling standard deviation to estimate the variance of the return. This is the standard deviation calculated using a fixed number of the most recent observations, for example 22 business days of data. It assumes that the variance of tomorrow's return can be describe as an equally weighted average of the squared residuals from the last 22 days. The assumption of equal weights seems unrealistic, since the more recent events must be more relevant and therefore should have higher weights. The ARCH model proposed by Engle [1982] let these weights be parameters to be estimated. Thus, the model allowed the data to determine the best weights to use in forecasting the variance.

Let X_t be the log return of a particular stock or the market portfolio from time $t-1$ to time t. Let I_{t-1} denotes the past information set containing the realized values of all relevant variables up to time $t-1$.

Suppose investors know the information in I_{t-1} when they make their investment decision at time $t-1$. Then the relevant expected return μ_t to the investors is the conditional expected value of X_t, given I_{t-1}, i.e.

$$\mu_t = E(X_t|I_{t-1}).$$

The relevant expected volatility σ_t^2 to the investors is conditional variance of X_t, given I_{t-1}, i.e.

$$\sigma_t^2 = Var(X_t|I_{t-1}).$$

Then

$$\epsilon_t = X_t - \mu_t$$

is the unexpected return at time t.

In the paper Engle and Ng [1993] ϵ_t is treated as a collective measure of news at time t. A positive ϵ_t (an unexpected increase in price) suggests the arrival of good news, while a negative ϵ_t (an unexpected decrease in price) suggests the arrival of bad news. Further, a large value of $|\epsilon_t|$ implies that the news is "significant" or "big" in the sense that it produces a large unexpected change in price.

Engle Engle [1982] suggests that the conditional variance σ_t^2 can be modeled as a function of the lagged ϵ's. That is, the predictable volatility is dependent on past news. The most detailed model he develops is the q-th order autoregressive conditional heteroscedasticity model, the ARCH(q).

Let (u_n) be a sequence of i.i.d. random variables such that $u_t \sim N(0, 1)$. A process (ϵ_t) is said to be the ARCH(q) process if

$$\epsilon_t = \sigma_t u_t, t \in \mathbb{Z}, \tag{5.1}$$

where (σ_t) is a nonnegative process such that

$$\sigma_t^2 = \alpha_0 + \sum_{i=1}^{q} \alpha_i \epsilon_{t-i}^2,$$

where $\alpha_0, \alpha_1, \ldots, \alpha_q$ are constant parameters. The effect of a return shock i periods ago ($i \leq q$) on current volatility is governed by the parameter α_i. Normally, one would expect that $\alpha_i < \alpha_j$ for $i > j \geq 1$. That is, the older the news, the less effect it has on current volatility. In an ARCH(q) model, old news which arrived at the market more than q periods ago has no effect at all on current volatility.

5.3   GARCH(p, q) Model

5.3.1   Model Description

Bollerslev (Bollerslev [1986]) generalizes the ARCH(q) model to the GARCH(p, q) model in the following way.

Let (u_n) be a sequence of i.i.d. random variables such that $u_t \sim N(0, 1)$.

A process (ϵ_t) is said to be the generalized autoregressive conditionally heteroscedastic or GARCH(p, q) process if

$$\epsilon_t = \sigma_t u_t, t \in \mathbb{Z}, \tag{5.2}$$

where (σ_t) is a nonnegative process such that

$$\sigma_t^2 = \alpha_0 + \alpha_1 \epsilon_{t-1}^2 + \ldots + \alpha_q \epsilon_{t-q}^2 + \beta_1 \sigma_{t-1}^2 + \ldots + \beta_p \sigma_{t-p}^2 =$$

$$= \alpha_0 + \sum_{i=1}^{q} \alpha_i \epsilon_{t-i}^2 + \sum_{j=1}^{p} \beta_j \sigma_{t-j}^2 \quad (5.3)$$

and

$$\alpha_i > 0, \ i = 0, \ldots, q, \ \beta_j > 0, \ j = 1, \ldots, p. \quad (5.4)$$

The conditions (5.4) on parameters ensure strong positivity of the conditional variance (5.3).

Let B denotes the lag-operator, i.e.

$$B y_t = y_{t-1}, \ B^k = B(B^{k-1}).$$

Then we can write (5.3) in the following way:

$$\sigma_t^2 = \alpha_0 + \alpha(B) \epsilon_t^2 + \beta(B) \sigma_t^2 \quad (5.5)$$

where

$$\alpha(B) = \alpha_1 B + \alpha_2 B^2 + \ldots + \alpha_q B^q,$$

$$\beta(B) = \beta_1 B + \beta_2 B^2 + \ldots + \beta_p B^p.$$

Suppose that the roots of the characteristic equation

$$1 - \beta_1 x - \beta_2 x^2 - \ldots - \beta_p x^p = 0$$

lie outside the unit circle and the process (ϵ_t) is stationary. Then we can write (5.3) as

$$\sigma_t^2 = \frac{\alpha_0}{1 - \beta(B)} + \frac{\alpha(B)}{1 - \beta(B)} \epsilon_t^2 = \alpha_0^* + \sum_{i=1}^{\infty} \delta_t \epsilon_{t-i}^2, \quad (5.6)$$

where $\alpha_0^* = \frac{\alpha_0}{1-\beta_1}$, and δ_i are coefficient of B^i in expansion of $\frac{\alpha(B)}{1-\beta(B)}$.

It follows from (5.6) that the GARCH(p, q) process can be considered as an ARCH process of infinite order with a fractional structure of the coefficients.

From (5.2) it is obvious that the GARCH(1,1) process is weakly stationary if the process (σ_t^2) is weakly stationary. So if we want to study the properties and higher order moments of GARCH(1,1) process it is enough to do so for the process (σ_t^2).

It was mentioned by Bollerslev [1992] GARCH(1,1) is more preferable in most cases as compared to GARCH(p, q). We recall that a process (ϵ_t) is said to be the generalized autoregressive conditionally heteroscedastic or GARCH(1,1) process if $\epsilon_t = \sigma_t u_t, t \in \mathbb{Z}$, where (σ_t) is a nonnegative process such that

$$\sigma_t^2 = \omega + \alpha \epsilon_{t-1}^2 + \beta \sigma_{t-1}^2.$$

In the model, α reflects the influence of random deviations in the previous period on σ_t, whereas β measures the part of the realized variance in the previous period that is carried over into the current period. The sizes of the parameters α and β determine the short-run dynamics of the resulting volatility time series. Large GARCH error coefficients, α, mean that volatility reacts intensely to market movements. Large GARCH lag coefficients, β, indicate that shocks to conditional variance take a long time die out, so volatility is persistent.

We will use a GARCH model of order 1 since it has been shown to provide a abstemious representation of the conditional variance. GARCH(1,1) was carefully tested (see e.g. the survey Bollerslev [1992]). Also Hansen and Lunde (Hansen and Lunde [2001]) "found no evidence that a GARCH(1,1) is outperformed by more sophisticated models" for prediction of variance of stock returns.

5.3.2   Maximum likelihood estimation of GARCH model

To calibrate the GARCH(p, q) model we can use different methods including the least-square estimator or generalized moment method, but in this work we will apply the maximum likelihood approach.

The subsection describes quasi-maximum likelihood estimation (QML) of model (5.2), (5.3), (5.4). The vector of model parameters is

$$\theta = (\alpha_0, \alpha_1, \ldots, \alpha_q, \beta_1, \ldots, \beta_p)^T.$$

Since the errors are assumed to be conditionally i.i.d. normal, maximum likelihood is a natural choice to estimate the unknown parameters, θ. We will assume that θ belongs to the set

$$\Theta := \{(\alpha_0, \alpha_1, \ldots, \alpha_q, \beta_1, \ldots, \beta_p)^T : \alpha_0 \geq 0, \ \alpha_i > 0, \ \beta_j > 0\}.$$

Denote

$$\theta^* = (\alpha_0^*, \alpha_1^*, \ldots, \alpha_q^*, \beta_1^*, \ldots, \beta_p^*)^T$$

the vector of the true values of parameters. The aim is to find θ^* that maximize a QML function given an observation sequence

$$\epsilon_0, \ldots, \epsilon_n$$

of length n.

Define the sequence $(\tilde{\sigma}_1, \ldots, \tilde{\sigma}_n)$ by recursion:

$$\tilde{\sigma}_t^2 = \alpha_0 + \sum_{i=1}^{q} \alpha_i \epsilon_{t-i}^2 + \sum_{j=1}^{p} \beta_j \tilde{\sigma}_{t-j}^2, \ 1 \leq t \leq n,$$

where $\epsilon_{1-q}, \ldots, \epsilon_0$ and $\tilde{\sigma}_{1-p}, \ldots, \tilde{\sigma}_0$ are an initial values of ϵ's and σ's respectively.

Given the initial values, the Gaussian quasi-likelihood function can be written as follows

$$L_n(\theta) = L_n(\theta; \epsilon_1, \ldots, \epsilon_n) = \prod_{t=1}^{n} \frac{1}{\sqrt{2\pi\tilde{\sigma}_t^2}} \exp\left(-\frac{\epsilon_t^2}{2\tilde{\sigma}_t^2}.\right)$$

The optimal estimation of θ is defined by

$$\tilde{\theta} = \arg\max_{\theta \in \Theta} L_n(\theta) = \arg\max_{\theta \in \Theta} F_n(\theta),$$

where

$$F_n(\theta) := -\sum_{t=1}^{n} \left(\frac{\epsilon_t^2}{\tilde{\sigma}_t^2} + \log \tilde{\sigma}_t^2\right)$$

is log quasi-likelihood function (constant terms are ignored).

5.4   Asymmetric GARCH models

The asymmetric effect was mentioned for the first time by Black in the paper Black [1976] and was also studied by Kenneth R. French, G. William Schwert and Robert F. Stambaugh (French et al. [1987]), D. Nelson (Nelson [1990]), and G. William Schwert (Schwert [1990]).

To capture the asymmetric effects a few models were introduced since then. In this section we will describe the the following most commonly used asymmetric GARCH models:

1. Exponential GARCH (EGARCH) model;

2. The Quadratic GARCH (QGARCH) model;

3. The Glosten-Jagannathan-Runkle GARCH (GJR-GARCH) model;

4. The Threshold GARCH (TGARCH) model.

We will consider the problem of calibration of this models as well.

5.4.1   EGARCH Model

Exponential GARCH (EGARCH) model can be defined by D. Nelson as follows Nelson [1991]:

$$\log(\sigma_t^2) = \alpha_0 + \sum_{i=1}^{q} \left(\gamma_i \frac{\epsilon_{t-i}}{\sigma_{t-i}} + \alpha_i \left| \frac{\epsilon_{t-i}}{\sigma_{t-i}} \right| \right) + \sum_{j=1}^{p} \beta_j \log(\sigma_{t-j}^2),$$

where α_0, α_i, β_j, γ_i are parameters.

The EGARCH model is asymmetric because the levels of $\frac{\epsilon_{t-i}}{\sigma_{t-i}}$'s are included with coefficients γ_i, which are typically negative. Thus positive return shocks generate less volatility than negative return shocks.

The paper Engle and Ng [1993] pointed out that

1. The EGARCH model allows good news and bad news to have a different impact on volatility, while the standard GARCH model does not;

2. The EGARCH model allows big news to have a greater impact on volatility than the standard GARCH model.

EGARCH(1,1) model can be written as

$$\log(\sigma_t^2) = \alpha_0 + \beta \log(\sigma_{t-1}^2) + \gamma \frac{\epsilon_{t-1}}{\sigma_{t-1}} + \alpha_1 \frac{|\epsilon_{t-1}|}{\sigma_{t-1}},$$

where $\alpha_0, \alpha_1, \beta, \gamma$ are parameters.

5.4.2   QGARCH model

The Quadratic GARCH (QGARCH) model was invented and studied by Sentana in 1995 Sentana [1995]. The model captures the asymmetric effects of positive and negative shocks. QGARCH(1,1) model may be defined as follows.

Let (u_n) be a sequence of i.i.d. random variables such that $u_t \sim N(0, 1)$.

A process (ϵ_t) is said to be QGARCH(1,1) process if

$$\epsilon_t = \sigma_t u_t, t \in \mathbb{Z}, \tag{5.7}$$

where (σ_t) is a nonnegative process such that

$$\sigma_t^2 = \alpha_0 + \alpha_1 \epsilon_{t-1}^2 + \beta_1 \sigma_{t-1}^2 + \gamma_1 \epsilon_{t-1} \tag{5.8}$$

and

$$\alpha_0, \alpha_1, \beta_1, \gamma_1 > 0. \tag{5.9}$$

Note that QGARCH model can be reduced to the well-studied GARCH(1,1) model for $\gamma = 0$, and the model captures the leverage effect for $\gamma < 0$.

5.4.3   GJR–GARCH model

The Glosten-Jagannathan-Runkle GARCH (GJR-GARCH) model was developed by Glosten, Jagannathan and Runkle in 1993 Glosten et al. [1993]. The model is similar to QGARCH in the sense of capturing of asymmetry in the ARCH process.

As it is above let (u_n) denotes a sequence of i.i.d. random variables such that $u_t \sim N(0,1)$.

A process (ϵ_t) is said to be GJR–GARCH(1,1) process if

$$\epsilon_t = \sigma_t u_t, t \in \mathbb{Z}, \tag{5.10}$$

where (σ_t) is a nonnegative process such that

$$\sigma_t^2 = \alpha_0 + \alpha_1 \epsilon_{t-1}^2 + \beta_1 \sigma_{t-1}^2 + \gamma_1 \epsilon_{t-1}^2 \chi_{t-1}, \tag{5.11}$$

where $\alpha_0, \alpha_1, \beta_1, \gamma_1 > 0$ and

$$\chi_{t-1} = 0 \text{ if } \epsilon_{t-1} \geq 0, \text{ and } \chi_{t-1} = 1 \text{ if } \epsilon_{t-1} < 0. \tag{5.12}$$

5.4.4   Threshold GARCH model

The Threshold GARCH (TGARCH) model was studied by Zakoian in 1994 (Zakoian [1994]). TGARCH model is indeed similar to GJR–GARCH models defined in the previous subsection. The specification of TGARCH model is one on conditional standard deviation instead of conditional variance. Here is definition of the model. A process (ϵ_t) is said to be TGARCH(1,1) process if

$$\epsilon_t = \sigma_t u_t, t \in \mathbb{Z}, \tag{5.13}$$

where (σ_t) is a nonnegative process such that

$$\sigma_t = \alpha_0 + \alpha^+ \epsilon_{t-1}^+ + \alpha^- \epsilon_{t-1}^- + \beta_1 \sigma_{t-1}, \tag{5.14}$$

where

$$\epsilon_{t-1}^+ = \begin{cases} \epsilon_{t-1}, & \text{if } \epsilon_{t-1} \geq 0, \\ 0, & \text{if } \epsilon_{t-1} < 0. \end{cases} \tag{5.15}$$

and

$$\bar{\epsilon}_{t-1} = \begin{cases} \epsilon_{t-1}, & \text{if } \epsilon_{t-1} \leq 0, \\ 0, & \text{if } \epsilon_{t-1} > 0. \end{cases} \tag{5.16}$$

5.4.5 Calibration of Asymmetric Models

Given an observation sequence

$$\epsilon_0, \ldots, \epsilon_n$$

of length n, define the sequence $(\tilde{\sigma}_1, \ldots, \tilde{\sigma}_n)$

1. in EGARCH(1,1) model by

$$\log(\tilde{\sigma}_t^2) = \alpha_0 + \beta \log(\tilde{\sigma}_{t-1}^2) + \gamma \frac{\epsilon_{t-1}}{\tilde{\sigma}_{t-1}} + \alpha_1 \frac{|\epsilon_{t-1}|}{\tilde{\sigma}_{t-1}},$$

   where $\alpha_0, \alpha_1, \beta, \gamma$ are estimated (unknown) parameters;

2. in QGARCH(1,1) model by

$$\tilde{\sigma}_t^2 = \alpha_0 + \alpha_1 \epsilon_{t-1}^2 + \beta_1 \tilde{\sigma}_{t-1}^2 + \gamma_1 \epsilon_{t-1}$$

   where $\alpha_0, \alpha_1, \beta_1, \gamma_1 > 0$ are estimated (unknown) parameters;

3. in GJR-GARCH(1,1) model by

$$\tilde{\sigma}_t^2 = \alpha_0 + \alpha_1 \epsilon_{t-1}^2 + \beta_1 \tilde{\sigma}_{t-1}^2 + \gamma_1 \epsilon_{t-1}^2 \chi_{t-1},$$

   where $\alpha_0, \alpha_1, \beta_1, \gamma_1 > 0$ are estimated (unknown) parameters and χ_{t-1} is defined in (5.12).

4. in Threshold GARCH(1,1) model by

$$\tilde{\sigma}_t = \alpha_0 + \alpha^+ \epsilon_{t-1}^+ + \alpha^- \bar{\epsilon}_{t-1} + \beta_1 \tilde{\sigma}_{t-1},$$

   where $\alpha_0, \alpha^+, \alpha^-, \beta_1$ are estimated (unknown) parameters and $\epsilon_{t-1}^+, \bar{\epsilon}_{t-1}$ are defined in (5.15), (5.16).

If we assume that the likelihood function is Gaussian, then the log-likelihood function can be written as

$$F_n(\theta) := -\sum_{t=1}^{n} \left(\frac{\epsilon_t^2}{\tilde{\sigma}_t^2} + \log \tilde{\sigma}_t^2 \right)$$

(constant terms are ignored). The maximum likelihood estimator of θ is defined by

$$\tilde{\theta} = \arg \max_{\theta \in \Theta} F_n(\theta).$$

It is worth noting that estimates obtained by maximizing the log likelihood of a normal distribution are strongly consistent (although they are not efficient). Recall that an estimator has the property of strong consistency if parameter estimates converge to the true parameters (even assuming the wrong conditional distribution).

If the GARCH model correspond the true data process, then the parameters of the GARCH model are chosen such that the conditional expectation of the generalized error 0. The normal distribution has the property that these parameters will correspond to those of the original data process even if the conditional distribution is incorrect.

The assumption that the errors are conditionally normal has some advantages: estimation is quite simple and parameters are consistent for the true parameters. But the alternative (non–normal) distributions are more useful in application to Value-at-Risk in which case the choice of density may lead to a better prediction capacity.

Some researchers estimate GARCH models assuming an alternative distribution (see, for example Bollerslev [1987]). It gave a better approximation to the conditional distribution of the standardized returns. Moreover, in the case of MLE, the estimates are fully efficient.

5.5   Empirical Study

5.5.1   Data Description

The data set we analyzed in this work is stock market closing daily prices of the General Electric Company (GEC.L)

The sample period is from January 2, 2008 to December 31, 2010. Total number of observations is 757. Data set are taken from UK Stock Market FTSE100 and downloaded from Yahoo!Finance site. The sample is divided in twelve parts for two purposes:

- *In-sample estimation procedure.* The twelve parts of observations are used as in-sample data. The first data set consists of data from January 2, 2008 to December 31, 2009. The i-th data set represents data from the first day of i-th month of 2008 to the last day of $i - 1$-th month of 2010. The twelfth data set is from January 2, 2009 to December 31, 2010. We will estimate parameters of models on each of this data sets.

- *Out-of-sample evaluation.* The remaining observations (from January 2, 2010 to December 31, 2010) are used as out-of-sample for forecast evaluation purposes. We will use the parameters obtained on previous step to estimate predictive properties of models. We divide the data set (from January 2, 2010 to December 31, 2010) on twelve one-month length parts. The data of i-th month of 2010 will be used to estimate the forecast properties of model which parameters was obtained based on i-th in-sample data set.

Figure 5.1 presents the General Electric prices movement during the period from January 2, 2008 to December 31, 2010.

Due to significant changes in the level of prices from date to date, it is more appropriate to base volatility measures on percentage return, rather than absolute price movement. Returns are calculated by

$$r_t = 100 \log \frac{p_t}{p_{t-1}},$$

Table 5.1: Descriptive statistics of General Electric company stock market closing daily prices (January 2, 2008 - December 31, 2010)

Form	To	Size	Mean	Std. dev.	Min	Max
02/01/2008	31/12/2010	757	19.29868	7.514138	6.66	38.43

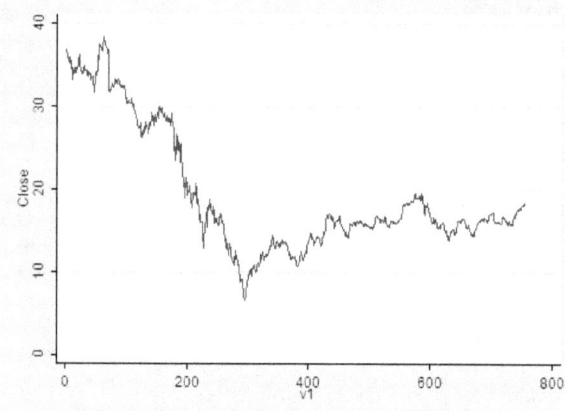

Figure 5.1: Historical movement of General Electric stock market closing daily prices (January 2, 2008 - December 31, 2010)

where p_t and P_{t-1} are closing price on dates t and $t-1$ respectively. The reason for using natural logarithm of trading volume is to improve the normality of the series in order to better fit into the GARCH-type models.

The descriptive statistics of GE stock log returns shows the stylized fact that the returns series is not close to normality as reflected by kurtosis value. Returns ranges from -13.68411 to 17.98444 and mean of returns is not statistically different from zero at 5% level. Historical movement of the GE log returns one can find in Figure 5.2. Time series of returns appears to show the signs of ARCH effects in that the amplitude of the returns varies over time. Figure 5.4 presents the histogram of the GE log returns during the period.

The positive skewness implies that returns distribution has a higher probability of earning positive returns. Kurtosis value is 7.708553 and this is much larger than 3. This shows that for our returns series, the distribution has fatter tails and sharper peaks at the center compared to the normal distribution (see Fig. 5.4). That behavior is known to occur in financial markets often.

The Jarque–Bera test statistics was also found to have a high value at significant 1% level and therefore we have to reject the null hypothesis of normality. Shapiro–Wilk W test also rejects the hypothesis of normal distribution of the data.

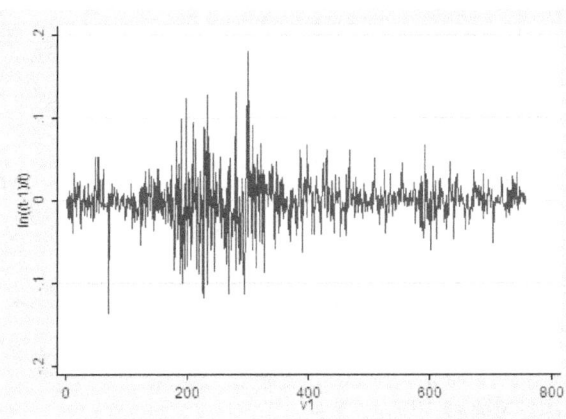

Figure 5.2: Historical movement of log returns of the General Electric stock market closing daily prices (January 2, 2008 - December 31, 2010)

We used the test of the white noise process given by the Ljun-Box-Pierce portmanteau test statistics in order to test the hypothesis of independence. The first-order autocorrelations of our series are small and statistically nonsignificant and returns do not have first-order autocorrelations. The computed statistical values of Ljung-Box-Pierce for lags 10 and 20 for our returns series (denoted by Q(10) and Q(20) respectively) are relatively large. The Q(10) and Q(20) test statistic reject

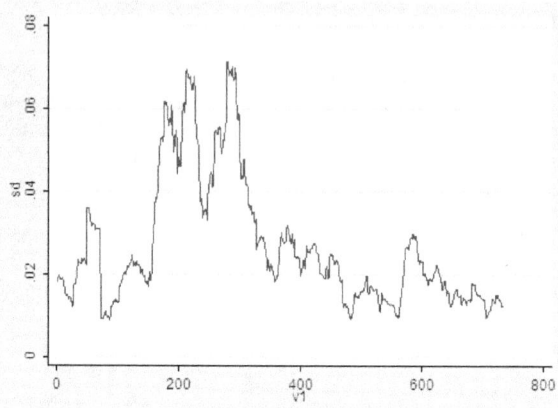

Figure 5.3: The rolling standard deviation of log returns of the General Electric stock market closing daily prices (January 2, 2008 - December 31, 2010), with 21 days rolling window

the null hypothesis of uncorrelated price changes, suggesting a slowly decaying autoregressive effect. Thus, the null hypothesis of strict white noise is rejected.

5.5.2   Empirical results

Kupiec's test.

Since the late 1990's a variety of tests have been proposed that can be used to estimate the accuracy of a VaR model. To compare the performance of models, in this work we will use the approach developed by Kupiec Kupiec [1995].

The idea is quite simple. This tests are concerned with whether or not the reported VaR is violated more (or less) than $\alpha100\%$ of the time. Kupiec finds a proportion of failures that examines how many times an asset's VaR is violated

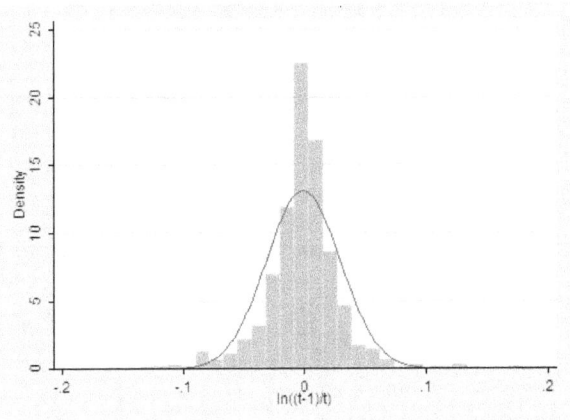

Figure 5.4: Histogram of log returns of the General Electric stock market closing daily prices (January 2, 2008 - December 31, 2010)

over a given span of time. If the number of violations differs considerably from $\alpha 100\%$ of the sample, then the accuracy of the underlying risk model is called into question.

Denote by y_t the actual losses at the day t. Consider the event that the loss on a portfolio exceeds its reported VaR (estimated by a model), VaR_t, i.e. $y_t > VaR_t$. Let $\{I_t\}$, $1 \le t \le T$, be the sequence with

$$I_t = \begin{cases} 1, & \text{if } y_t > VaR_t, \\ 0, & \text{if } y_t \le VaR_t. \end{cases} \tag{5.17}$$

Denote by

$$N = \sum_{t=1}^{T} I_t \tag{5.18}$$

the number of such violations.

Kupiec's test statistic has the form Kupiec [1995]

$$L = 2log\left(\left(\frac{1-N/T}{1-\alpha}\right)^{T-N}\left(\frac{N/T}{\alpha}\right)^{N}\right)$$

The intervals of non-rejection for some α is given in Table 5.2.

Table 5.2: The intervals of non-rejection regions for Kupiec's test

α	$T = 250$	$T = 500$	$T = 750$	$T = 1000$
5%	$7 \leq N \leq 19$	$17 \leq N \leq 35$	$25 \leq N \leq 49$	$38 \leq N \leq 64$
1%	$1 \leq N \leq 6$	$2 \leq N \leq 9$	$3 \leq N \leq 13$	$5 \leq N \leq 16$

Christoffersen Christoffersen [1998] points out that the problem of determining the accuracy of a VaR model can be reduced to the problem of determining whether the sequence of violations, $\{I_t\}$, $1 \leq t \leq T$, satisfies two properties:

1. *Unconditional coverage property.* The unconditional coverage property places a restriction on how often VaR violations may occur. The probability of realizing a loss in excess of the reported VaR_t must be precisely $\alpha100\%$ or in terms of the previous notation, $P(I_{t+1}(\alpha)) = \alpha$. If it is the case that losses in excess of the reported VaR occur more frequently than 100% of the time then this would suggest that the reported VaR measure systematically understates the portfolio's actual level of risk. The opposite finding of too few VaR violations would alternatively signal an overly conservative VaR measure.

2. *Independence property.* The independence property places a strong restriction on the ways in which these violations may occur. Specifically, any two elements of the hit sequence, $I_{t+j}(\alpha), I_{t+k}(\alpha)$ must be independent from each other.

The group of competing GARCH models (ARCH, GARCH, TGARCH, GJR-GARCH) are estimated using quasi-maximum likelihood method.

Table 5.3 presents autocorrelations, partial autocorrelations, and Portmanteau (Q) statistics. It shows that there is no autocorrelation in GE stock returns time series. Therefore, we do not include autoregressive and moving average terms in mean equation. We will assume $\mu = \mathbb{E}(r_t)$.

Table 5.3: The autocorrelations, partial autocorrelations and Portmanteau (Q) statistics for GE log returns of the closing daily prices

LAG	Auto. corr	PAC	Q	$Prob > Q$
1	-0.016	-0.016	0.19481	0.6589
2	0.023	0.0228	0.59748	0.7418
3	0.0066	0.0074	0.63086	0.8893
4	0.0414	0.0412	1.9398	0.7468
5	-0.0683	-0.0675	5.4942	0.3586
6	0.0676	0.0642	8.9892	0.1742
7	0.0126	0.0167	9.1113	0.2448
8	-0.0441	-0.0478	10.601	0.2253
9	-0.0595	-0.0572	13.32	0.1486
10	0.0874	0.0795	19.19	0.0379

The following estimates of parameters were obtained using the statistical environment R:

- ARCH(1) model parameters's estimation of returns for the GE stock market closing daily prices (January 2, 2008 - December 31, 2010), $\sigma_t^2 = \alpha_0 + \alpha_1 \epsilon_{t-1}^2$,

- GARCH(1,1) model parameters's estimation of returns of the GE company closing daily prices (January 2, 2008 - December 31, 2010, $\sigma_t^2 = \omega + \alpha \epsilon_{t-1}^2 + \beta \sigma_{t-1}^2$,

- Threshold GARCH(1,1) model parameters's estimation of returns of the GE company closing daily prices (January 2, 2008 - December 31, 2010), $\sigma_t = \alpha_0 + \alpha^+ \epsilon_{t-1}^+ + \alpha^- \epsilon_{t-1}^- + \beta_1 \sigma_{t-1}$,

- GJR–GARCH(1,1) model parameters's estimation of returns of the GE company closing daily prices (January 2, 2008 - December 31, 2010), $\sigma_t^2 = \alpha_0 + \alpha_1 \epsilon_{t-1}^2 + \beta_1 \sigma_{t-1}^2 + \gamma_1 \epsilon_{t-1}^2 \chi_{t-1}$, where $\chi_{t-1} = 0$ if $\epsilon_{t-1} \geq 0$, and $\chi_{t-1} = 1$ if $\epsilon_{t-1} < 0$,

Notice that the coefficients sum up to a number less than one, which is required
to have a mean reverting variance process. Since the sum is very close to one, this
process only mean reverts slowly.

Figure shows the values of conditional variance of General Electric stock market
closing daily prices, based on 1-year GARCH model, 1-day prediction.

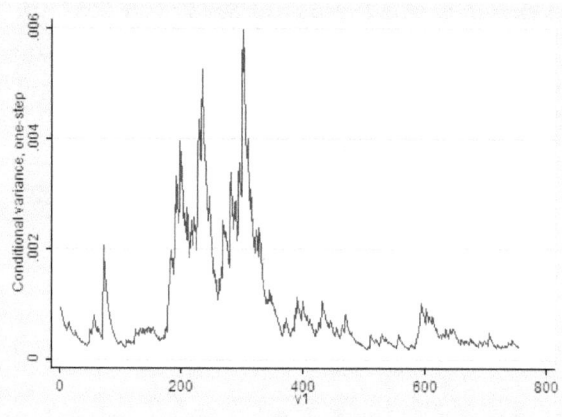

Figure 5.5: Prediction of conditional variance of General Electric stock market closing daily prices (January 2, 2008 - December 31, 2009), based on 1-year
GARCH model

Thus, we have estimates of parameters for ARCH, GARCH, TGARCH, GJR-
GARCH models for all 24 in-sample datasets. Using these estimated parameters, we can forecast the one day ahead volatility for each day of out-of-sample
datasets. To do so we put the values of the estimated parameters in the formula
for their respective models. For example, to predict the value of σ_t using Threshold GARCH(1,1) model we have to substitute the estimated values of parame-
ters α_0, α^+, α^- and β_1 in the equation of $TGARCH(1,1)$ model at time $t = k$,
$1 \le k \le 21$:

$$\sigma_k = \alpha_0 + \alpha^+ \epsilon^+_{k-1} + \alpha^- \epsilon^-_{k-1} + \beta_1 \sigma_{k-1},$$

where ϵ^+_{k-1} and ϵ^-_{k-1} are positive and negative part of the value of the squared return of the previous day respectively. Further the value of variance σ_k at time k is used to forecast the volatility at time $k+1$ using out-of-sample data set:

$$\sigma_{k+1} = \alpha_0 + \alpha^+ \epsilon^+_k + \alpha^- \epsilon^-_k + \beta_1 \sigma_k.$$

Thus, we can forecast volatility for up to 21st day. The same way is used for the volatility forecast by $ARCH(1,1), GARCH(1,1), GJR - GARCH(1,1)$ models.

The same procedure we use for volatility forecast for each of 12 out-of-sample datasets. Hence volatility is forecasted for 251 days from $04/01/10$ to $31/12/10$ using each of 4 models, for all of 12 out-of-sample datasets.

Then $VaR_t(\alpha), 506 \le t \le 757$ is calculated by

$$VaR_t(\alpha) = f(\alpha) \cdot \sigma_t,$$

where $\alpha = 0.05$ or 0.01 is confidence level and σ_t is estimated volatility for the day t.

Thus VaR is forecasted using different models for the whole of the out of sample period of 251 days from date $04/01/10$ to $31/12/10$.

The values of $VaR_t(\alpha)$ can be used for the purpose of judging the performance of the volatility models. To apply the unconditional coverage of Kupiec Kupiec [1995] it is necessary to find the number of violations by using (5.17). Non-rejection region one can find in the Table 5.2.

Number of VaR violations of each model for 1-year length of in-sample datasets is given in Table 5.4 and Table 5.5. Number of VaR violations of each model for 2-year length of in-sample datasets is given in Table 5.6 and Table 5.7.

Table 5.4 and Table 5.5 show that for 95% and 99% confidence level respectively, all models calibrated on 1-year dataset cannot be rejected.

On the other hand, Table 5.6 and Table 5.7 show that for 95% and 99% confidence level, all models calibrated on 2-year dataset must be rejected, since they over predict the risk and the models falls out of the non-rejection region.

Table 5.4: Numbers of failures with 95% confidence level, 1-year length of dataset

Model	Length	Conf	Failures	Freq	%
ARCH(1,1)	1 year	95%	8	251	3.17
GARCH(1,1)	1 year	95%	9	251	3.57
GJR-GARCH	1 year	95%	10	251	3.98
TGARCH	1 year	95%	10	251	3.98

Table 5.5: Numbers of failures with 99% confidence level, 1-year length of dataset

Model	Length	Conf	Failures	Freq	%
ARCH(1,1)	1 year	99%	2	251	0.79
GARCH(1,1)	1 year	99%	3	251	1.19
GJR-GARCH	1 year	99%	3	251	1.19
TGARCH	1 year	99%	3	251	1.19

Christoffersen' s interval forecast test

Christoffersen (1998) proposed a test of conditional coverage. He extends the Kupiec's test to examines whether the probability of an exception on any day depends on the outcome of the previous day.

Thus Christoffersen's test not only covers the violation rate but the independence of exception also. If the model is accurate, then an exception today should not depend on whether or not an exception occurred on the previous day.

Define an indicator variable

$$I_t = \begin{cases} 1, & \text{if violation occurs in the day } t, \\ 0, & \text{if no violation occurs in the day } t, \end{cases}$$

i.e. I_t gets a value of 1 if VaR is exceeded and value of 0 if VaR is not exceeded.

Denote by n_{ij} the number of days when condition $I_t = j$ occurred assuming that condition $I_t = i$ occurred on the previous day.

To illustrate, the outcome can be displayed in a table:

Table 5.6: Numbers of failures with 95% confidence level, 2-year length of in-sample dataset

Model	Length	Conf	Failures	Freq	%
ARCH(1,1)	2 year	95%	1	251	0.40
GARCH(1,1)	2year	95%	1	251	0.40
GJR-GARCH	2 year	95%	1	251	0.40
TGARCH	2 year	95%	2	251	0.79

Table 5.7: Numbers of failures with 99% confidence level, 2-year length of in-sample dataset

Model	Length	Conf	Failures	Freq	%
ARCH(1,1)	2 year	99%	0	251	0.00
GARCH(1,1)	2year	99%	0	251	0.00
GJR-GARCH	2 year	99%	0	251	0.00
TGARCH	2 year	99%	0	251	0.00

Let

$$\Pi_0 = \frac{n_{01}}{n_{00} + n_{01}}, \ \Pi_1 = \frac{n_{11}}{n_{10} + n_{11}}, \ \Pi = \frac{n_{01} + n_{11}}{n_{00} + n_{01} + n_{10} + n_{11}}$$

Thus, n_{11} presents the number of consecutive exceptions, Π_i is the probability of an exception assuming a state i on the previous day, and Π is the probability of an exception regardless of the previous dayís state. The probabilities are calculated from the observed data.

The test statistic for independence of exception is likelihood-ratio:

$$LR = -2\log \frac{(1 - \Pi)^{n_{00} + n_{10}} \Pi^{n_{01} + n_{11}}}{(1 - \Pi_0)^{n_{00}} \Pi_0^{n_{01}} (1 - \Pi_1)^{n_{10}} \Pi_1^{n_{11}}} \tag{5.19}$$

LR is also $\chi^2(1)$-distributed. If the value of the LR statistic is lower than the critical value of $\chi^2(1)$ distribution, the model passes the test. Higher values lead to rejection of the model.

	$I_{t-1} = 0$	$I_{t-1} = 1$	
$I_t = 0$	n_{00}	n_{10}	$n_{00} + n_{10}$
$I_t = 1$	n_{01}	n_{11}	$n_{01} + n_{11}$
	$n_{00} + n_{01}$	$n_{10} + n_{11}$	N

As an example, consider again the ARCH model results at 95% confidence level. The contingency table can be presented as follows

	$I_{t-1} = 0$	$I_{t-1} = 1$	
$I_t = 0$	235	7	235
$I_t = 1$	7	1	8
	235	8	250

In addition, we need to find the probabilities

$$\Pi_0 = \frac{4}{235 + 7} = 0.032089, \ \Pi_1 = \frac{1}{7 + 1} = 0.1250, \ \Pi = \frac{7 + 1}{235 + 7 + 7 + 1} = 0.0320$$

Plugging this data into the likelihood ratio statistic we obtain the test value:

$$LR = -2\log \frac{(1 - 0.0320)^{235+7} 0.0320^{7+1}}{(1 - 0.032089)^{235} 0.032089^7 (1 - 0.1250)^7 0.1250^1} = 1.3873$$

The critical value is the 95% percentile of the $\chi^2(1)$ distribution with one degree of freedom, 3.84. As the test statistic value remains below the critical value, the model is accepted.

Table 5.8 shows the input data for calculating the LR statistics for each models and confidence level.

Table 5.9 shows that for 95% and 99% confidence level, all models calibrated both on 1-year and on 2-year dataset cannot be rejected.

Table 5.8: Auxiliary data for the independence test

Model	Length	Conf	Fail.	n_{00}	n_{01}	n_{10}	n_{11}	Π_0	Π_1	Π
ARCH(1,1)	1 year	95%	8	235	7	7	1	0.032	0.125	0.032
GARCH(1,1)	1 year	95%	9	232	9	9	0	0.037	0.000	0.036
GJR-GARCH	1 year	95%	10	232	10	10	0	0.041	0.000	0.039
TGARCH	1 year	99%	10	232	10	10	0	0.041	0.000	0.039
ARCH(1,1)	1 year	99%	2	246	2	2	0	0.008	0.000	0.008
GARCH(1,1)	1 year	99%	3	244	3	3	0	0.012	0.000	0.012
GJR-GARCH	1 year	99%	3	244	3	3	0	0.012	0.000	0.012
TGARCH	1 year	99%	3	244	3	3	0	0.012	0.000	0.012
ARCH(1,1)	2 year	95%	1	248	1	1	0	0.004	0.000	0.004
GARCH(1,1)	2 year	95%	1	248	1	1	0	0.004	0.000	0.004
GJR-GARCH	2 year	95%	1	248	1	1	0	0.004	0.000	0.004
TGARCH	2 year	95%	2	246	2	2	0	0.008	0.000	0.008
ARCH(1,1)	2 year	99%	0	250	0	0	0	0.000	0.000	0.000
GARCH(1,1)	2 year	99%	0	250	0	0	0	0.000	0.000	0.000
GJR-GARCH	2 year	99%	0	250	0	0	0	0.000	0.000	0.000
TGARCH	2 year	99%	0	250	0	0	0	0.000	0.000	0.000

5.5.3 Summary

Backtesting procedure shows that the ARCH(1), GARCH (1, 1), TGARCH(1,1) and GJR-GARCH (1, 1) models calibrated on datasets of **1-year length** (January 2, 2009 - December 31, 2009) under the normal distribution performed well forecasting VaR both at 95% and 99% in 2010 year.

However, for 95% and 99% VaR estimations all the ARCH(1), GARCH (1, 1), TGARCH(1,1) and GJR-GARCH (1, 1) models calibrated on datasets of **2-year length** (January 2, 2008 - December 31, 2009) underestimated the risk and should be rejected.

It can be explained by huge difference in the level of volatility in 2008 crisis year compare with the one in 2009 year. The conclusion is that the ARCH(1), GARCH (1, 1), TGARCH(1,1) and GJR-GARCH (1, 1) models are highly sensitive to dataset they are calibrated on.

Table 5.9: Christoffersen's independence test resuls

Model	Length	Conf	LR	Critical Value	
ARCH(1,1)	1 year	95%	1.3873	3.84	Accepted
GARCH(1,1)	1 year	95%	0.6724	3.84	Accepted
GJR-GARCH	1 year	95%	0.8336	3.84	Accepted
TGARCH	1 year	99%	0.8336	6.63	Accepted
ARCH(1,1)	1 year	99%	0.0323	6.63	Accepted
GARCH(1,1)	1 year	99%	0.0729	6.63	Accepted
GJR-GARCH	1 year	99%	0.0729	6.63	Accepted
TGARCH	1 year	99%	0.0729	6.63	Accepted
ARCH(1,1)	2 year	95%	0.0080	3.84	Accepted
GARCH(1,1)	2 year	95%	0.0080	3.84	Accepted
GJR-GARCH	2 year	95%	0.0080	3.84	Accepted
TGARCH	2 year	95%	0.0323	3.84	Accepted
ARCH(1,1)	2 year	99%	0.0000	6.63	Accepted
GARCH(1,1)	2 year	99%	0.0000	6.63	Accepted
GJR-GARCH	2 year	99%	0.0000	6.63	Accepted
TGARCH	2 year	99%	0.0000	6.63	Accepted

Chapter 6

News Analytics

6.1 Introduction

Many investment companies in the U.S. and Europe have been using news analytics to improve the quality of its business. Interest in news analytics is related to the ability to predict changes of prices, volatility and trading volume on the stock market Tetlock [2007].

News analytics uses some methods and technics of data mining Kantardzic [2003] and relies on methods of computer science, artificial intelligence (including algorithms for natural language processing), financial engineering, mathematical statistics and mathematical modeling. News analytics software signalize traders about the most important events or send their output data directly to automated trading algorithms, which take into account this signals automatically during the trade.

This chapter is a short review of the tools, methods and providers of news analytics and mostly based on the book Mitra and Mitra [2011].

6.2   What is the News Analytics?

News analytics can be described as a measurement of the following quantitative and qualitative characteristics of news:

1. **The nature of news** (it determines the impact of news (positive or negative), i.e. how news affects stock prices change; it is believed that positive news about the company leads to a growth in the stock prices of its shares, and negative, on the contrary, can leads to decreasing);

2. **The impact of news** (it is characterized by the influence of news on the scale of the changes caused by the news);

3. **The relevance** (describes how the events, described in a news report, are connected with the trader's interest security);

4. **The novelty** (shows how much news is informative, usually it is inversely correlated with the number of references to events that are written in this news report, with other news).

News analysis is a relatively new tool designed to improve the trading strategies of investors. It is closely connected with the theory of behavioral finance and in some sense, is contrary to the classical economic theory.

Indeed, the famous "efficient markets hypothesis" states Samuelson [1965] that any available information is already reflected in share prices. This condition makes it impossible to attempt to outperform the market in a long period of time through the use of information available on the market. On the other hand, in the modern world, the intensity level of various news agencies is so high (for example, Thomson Reuters has more than 4000 messages per day) that the trader is unable on its own to handle this information flow. Events that are potentially change the situation on the stock exchange, may be lost or omitted in a huge stream of news. In this context, it is unlikely that at any one time all traders will be equally informed of all events affecting the price of certain stocks. That is why the news analytics is an effective tool to gain advantage over other market participants.

Knowing the characteristics of news in numerical indices one can use them in mathematical and statistical models and automated trading systems. Currently, the tools of the news analytics have been increasingly used by traders in the U.S. and Europe.

The process of news analysis in information systems is automated and usually includes the following steps:

1. collecting news from different sources;

2. preliminary analysis of news;

3. analysis of news-related expectations (sentiments), taking into account the current market situation;

4. designing and using of quantitative models.

The process of news analytics is described in more details in the following sections.

It worth be noted that managers of investment funds rarely use tools of news analytics, since they usually create investment portfolios for a long period of time, and in this case portfolio management does not suggest a frequent resale of securities.

6.2.1 Data Sources

News data can be obtained from various sources:

- **News sources of news agencies.** Until recently, the news had been spread by printed sources, radio, television and it was quite difficult to obtain an overall picture of the news flow. The Internet has changed the process of news analysis; the using of tagging and indexing has made possible their automatic processing.

- **Pre-news** is a raw information material which is used in the preparation of news by reporters. It can be obtained from different primary sources, for example, SEC reports, court documents, reports of various government agencies, business resources, company reports, announcements, industrial, and macroeconomic statistics.

- **Social media** (blogs, social networks, etc.). The quality of news from this type of sources can be vary highly, and this information is often useless. However, you can keep track (evaluate) the mood of a large number of these messages and apply results in trade strategies.

In addition, the financial news can be classified in terms of their expectations. Expected news come out at a scheduled time and often their contents can be predicted on the basis of pre-news. They have a structured format and generally include numeric data, which is convenient for automated analysis (e.g., usually all companies publish annual or quarterly financial reports in the same time). Macroeconomic reports have a strong influence on liquid markets (foreign exchange, futures, government bonds) and are widely used in the automatic trading. Speed and accuracy of processing of such information are important technological requirements. Reports of incomes and losses affect directly the change in stock prices and are widely used in trading strategies.

The main difficulties of the processing of financial information are associated with unexpected news, since the time of their appearance is unknown and, often they have a unstructured text format and do not contain numeric data. They are difficult to process quickly and efficiently, but they may contain information about the causes and consequences of the event. To analyze unexpected news one can use the artificial intelligence systems based on methods of natural language processing.

6.2.2 Pre–Analysis of News

News analytics evaluates the relevance, nature, novelty and the importance of news. The results of processing of news information are used to create signals for investors and traders. These signals can be combined with forecasts from other primary or processed sources.

6.2.3 Providers of News Analytics

In the world there are more than 50 providers of economic news. Bloomberg, Dow Jones and Thomson Reuters are the three largest of them. About 200 agencies are involved in providing of financial analytics.

The most well-known providers of news analytics and data are:

- **RavenPack** (http://www.ravenpack.com/) is one of the leading providers of real-time news analysis services. The company specializes in linguistic analysis of large volumes of news in real time from news providers. RavenPack News Scores measures the news sentiment and news flow of the global equity market based on all major investable equity securities. News scores include analytics on more than 27,000 companies in 83 countries and covers over 98% of the investable global market. All relevant news items about companies are classified and quantified according to their sentiment, relevance, topic, novelty, and market impact; the result is a data product that can be segmented into many distinct benchmarks and used in various applications. RavenPack is working with news feeds from the company Dow Jones.

- **Media Sentiment** (www.mediasentiment.com/) has a resource library of nearly 2,000,000 articles and it regularly searches and analyzes output from 6,000+ sources in near-real time to bring investors updated news media sentiment about publicly traded companies, both quickly and effortlessly.

- **Thomson Reuters News Analytics** (http://thomsonreuters.com) automatically analyzes news providing improved buy/hold/sell signals within milliseconds. The system can scan and analyze stories on thousands of companies in real-time and feed the results into your quantitative strategies. With its ability to track news sentiment over time, Thomson Reuters News Analytics provides a more comprehensive understanding of a companyís news coverage, helping to guide trading and investment decisions. It delivers unparalleled insight into a companyís market reputation, giving money managers a unique advantage. *Reuters NewsScope* and *Sentiment Analysis* are new software products, which provide financial news (interest rates, consumer price indices, etc.). These programs are designed for use in automated trading.

In the work we will use the Raven Pack sources of news analytics data. One can found the example of extract from the data in Table 6.1.

Table 6.1: Extracts from Raven Pack news analytics data

TIMESTAMP_UTC:	2010-01-21 21:20:08.297
COMPANY:	JP/7203 (Toyota Motor Corp.)
RP_COMPANY_ID:	CEC128
RELEVANCE:	100
EVENT CATEGORY:	product-recall
EVENT SENTIMENT (ESS):	29
NOVELTY (ENS):	100
NOVELTY ID (ENS_KEY):	D9592AD7D8E718...
COMPOSITE SENTIMENT (CSS):	50
WORD/PHRASE LEVEL (WLE):	50
PROJECTIONS BY COMPANY (PCM):	50
EDITORIALS & COMMENTARY (ECM):	50
REPORTS CORP ACTIONS (RCM):	50
VENTURE, CORPORATE, M& A (VCM):	50
NEWS IMPACT PROJECTION (NIP):	34
RP_STORY_ID:	D9592AD7D8E71...

6.3   Descriptive Statistics

Relevance calculated as a score between 0-100 that indicates how strongly related the company is to the underlying news. A Story with a great index value has great relevance. In our investigation we consider news with relevance score more than 90.

The Figure 6.1 presents the time plot of dynamics of number of news for all UK companies per day from January 2, 2005 to December 31, 2010.

We can see that news intensity is stable. In some days the number of news was much bigger than the mean level. The increase of number of news in such days may be caused by important macro economical events.

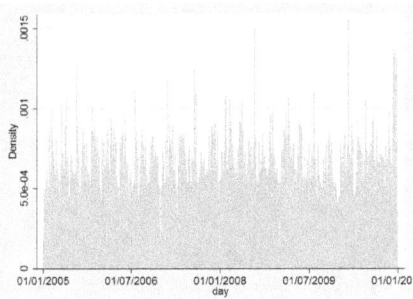

Figure 6.1: Total number of news for all UK companies per day (January 2, 2005 - December 31, 2010)

A preliminary analysis of RavenPack News historical dataset indicates strong seasonality on intahourly, intradaily, intraweekly, intrayearly timescales (Fig. 6.2, 6.3).

We use two fields ESS and CSS for calculating number of positive and negative news for each companies. ESS is (Event sentiment sentiment) a score between 0 and 100 that represents the news sentiment for a given company by measuring various proxies sampled from the news. The score is determined by systematically matching stories typically categorized by financial experts as having short-term positive or negative share price impact. A score range between 0-100 where higher values indicate more positive sentiment while lower values below 50 show negative sentiment.

CSS (composite sentiment scores) is sentiment score between 0 and 100 that represents the news sentiment of a given story by combining various sentiment analysis techniques. RavenPack recommended, as example, such way of using CSS scores: If CSS > 50 Then Positive Signal; If CSS < 50 Then Negative Signal; If CSS = 50 Then Neutral Signal.

The correlation coefficient between the indices is relatively small

$$cor(ESS, CSS) = 0.4643.$$

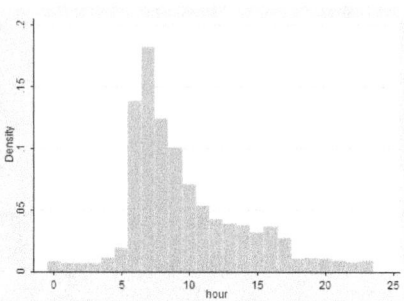

Figure 6.2: Intraday Arriving Time for Relevant News for UK Companies

Therefore, we compared the results obtained using both measures. We count the number of negative, neutral and positive news for a given company for each day.

The numbers of positive and negative ESS records for all UK companies are shown on Figures 6.4.

Table 6.2: Correlation Matrix

CSS positive	CSS negative	ESS positive	ESS negative
1			
0.85	1		
0.93	0.82	1	
0.82	0.90	0.79	1

The intensity of the flow of positive and negative news is strongly correlated. As a rule, positive and negative news comes in the same day. Perhaps this is due to inaccuracies in digitizing text messages.

Also we calculate day sentiment score as number of positive news record minus number of negative news records. In both cases there are a fall in the second half of 2008, and a gradual recovery in the first half of 2009.

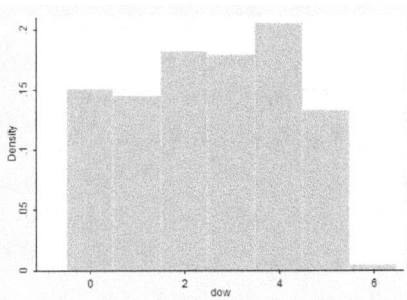

Figure 6.3: Seasonaity - Intra week Pattern for Relevant News for UK Companies

6.4   High Volatility Levels and News Flow Intensity

Abrupt and significant changes in the prices of financial instruments are not very frequent, but constitute an important part of contemporary (modern) financial markets. Conventional financial markets' wisdom claims that these price jumps represent a reaction of the financial markets to the news flow (changes in companies' positions, important business desicions).

News could contain information about current events or disclose some hidden (and not obvious to the market) events in corporate business decisions. In other words, news can make business events accessible to public (traders, market analytics, etc.).

This could make financial market participants to change their views of the current market state (situation), and consequently, lead to stock price movements.

It is hardly possible to construct an indicator capable of capturing the market significance of the particular news item. Nonetheless we believe that certain market state variables (for example, trading volume, Tauchen and Pitts [1983] could be used as latent factors capable of measuring the amount of relevant information flow.

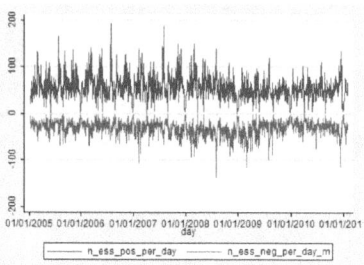

Figure 6.4: Number of Positive and Negative ESS and News Items for All UK Company

Hereinafter we assume that the significance of the currents news and information disclosure for the particular company has a measurable impact on the news flow intensity. It means that more news comes to the market in the days when importance for the company under consideration events occurs or relevant information pertaining to the company is disclosed. And vice versa hight intensity of the news on particular company signifies that some importance for this company events take place on this day, which could increase the possibility of the stock price jumps (well above the mean average level for the past days) on this day. Absence of the news arrives a conclusion that there is no important events on this day, and, consequently, the probability of the price jump is small.

We will try to find empirical evidence to the fact that overall number of news items and the amount of good and bad news through the day could be used to identify (or mark) days with the highest probability of price jumps in stock prices.

If the above stated hypothesis is true, then the following statements are also true: probability of extremely low or high return in correlated with the news flow intensity, days with the higher news intensity are caracterised by higher volatility.

Our calculations support the proposed hypothesis.

It should be noted that due to substantial fluctuations in volatility during the 5 year period under consideration, a number of problems arise when we try to classify a particular trading day as a day with abnormally high or low return rate.

We used a T-day standard deviation of return rate as an estimate for the volatility(sw_{it}). All further calculations use T=5.

The following criteria were introduced: rate of return was considered abnormally (extremely) low ($Neg.Jump_{it} = 1$) if $r_{it} < 1.96 * sw_{it}$ and extremely high ($Pos.Jump_{it} = 1$) if $r(it) > 1.96 * sw_{it}$. To enable comparison between different companies we used logarithms of the relative numbers of positive and negative news for the i-th company in day t as regressors:

New variables
$$N_{it}^+(adjusted) = ln((N_{it}^+ + 0.5)/\sum_t N_{it}^+)$$

$$N_{it}^-(adjusted) = ln((N_{it}^+ + 0.5)/\sum_t N_{it}^-)$$

were used as independent variables in binary choice models (logit regression):

$$Prob(Pos.Jump_{it} = 1) = \Lambda(\beta_0 + \beta_1 N_{it}^+ + \beta_2 N_{it}^-),$$
$$Prob(Neg.Jump_{it} = 1) = \Lambda(\gamma_0 + \gamma_1 N_{it}^- + \gamma_2 N_{it}^-),$$
where $\Lambda(X\beta) = e^{X\beta}/(1 + e^{X\beta})$.

Estimates of the logistic regression coefficient are given in Tables 6.3 and 6.4. Regression coefficients' significance proves the fact that high and low stock returns are more likely to occur on days with higher news intensity.

It should be also noted that the number of the positive news is the most significant predictor for the positive extremely high return (Table 6.3), and the number of the negative news - corresponds to the extreme loss (Table 6.4).

Table 6.3: Parameter estimates for panel logit model for positive abnormal returns

Pos.Jump	Coef.	Std. Err.	z	$Prob > \|z\|$	$95\%Conf.$	Interval
N^+	0.4787247	0.0242572	19.74	0.00	0.4311814	0.5262679
N^-	-0.1594172	0.027533	-5.79	0.00	-0.2133809	-0.1054535
cons	-1.22819	0.1582066	-7.76	0.00	-1.538269	-0.9181104

Table 6.4: Parameter estimates for panel logit model for negative abnormal returns

Neg.Jump	Coef.	Std. Err.	z	$Prob > \|z\|$	$95\%Conf.$	Interval
N^+	-0.0264089	0.03089	-0.85	0.393	-0.0869523	0.0341345
N^-	0.4555	0.0479	9.50	0.00	0.3616	0.5495
cons	-1.4076	0.2502	-5.63	0.00	-1.8980	-0.9173

Let's discuss some ways of verifying that volatility in marked days is really above the average. We are going to mark days when the registered number of the news was above the average. We have tried three different approaches to mark these days:

- The day is marked when there was at least one news on this day ($N_{it} > 0$);

- The day is marked when the relative number of news is bigger than certain threshold level c, i.e. $N_{it}/\sum_t N_{it} > c$;

- The day is marked when the number of the news items was greater than the upper bound for the confidence interval of the Poisson regression ($N_{it} > C_{it}$). We used dummy variables for days of the week, months of the year, certain years and periods with the maximum number of regular news per day as regressors (see Figure 6.5).

Remark. In weeks 17-18, 30-31, 44-45 of every year the number of the news items is generally above the average, which could be explained by the fact corporate financial reports are published on these days.

The first method has an obvious drawback. Having applied it, we usually end up with more than 50% days marked for some companies. Method 3 can take into

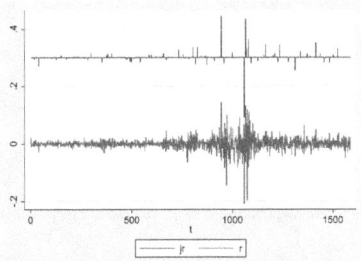

Figure 6.5: Historical movement of log returns of the HSBC Holding PLC stock market closing daily prices and log returns occurred in jump days predicted by Poisson regression (January 2, 2005 - December 31, 2010)

account seasonal factor in the news flow. Our own investigations have shown that methods 2 and 3 usually give similar results (similar days were marked).

If volatility levels in marked and not marked days are the same, then there is no evidence to the interdependence of the news flow intensity and price jumps in these days.

If volatility levels in marked and not marked days are different, we can explore another hypothesis, namely, that current volatility level consists of two components: smooth (or regular) and jumps.

The histogram (Figures 6.6) show that the yield spread greater in labeled days than in unlabeled days.

We use variance homogeneity test for hypothesis

$$\begin{cases} H_0 : \sigma_U^2 = \sigma_L^2, \\ H_1 : \sigma_U^2 < \sigma_L^2. \end{cases} \tag{6.1}$$

As an example we show the results of F-test for the homogeneity of variance for HSBC Plc. in Table 6.5.

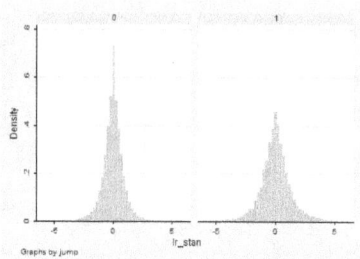

Figure 6.6: Density plot for returns for all FTSE100 companies for days with high level and low level news intensity

Table 6.5: F-test for the homogeneity of variance for HSBC Plc.

Group	Obs	Mean	Std. Dev.
1 (Labeled)	43	0.004	0.058
0 (Unlabeled)	1522	0.000	0.018
All	1565	0.000	0.020

$$F_{obs} = \frac{s_U^2}{s_L^2} = \frac{0.018^2}{0.058^2} = 0.138 < F(0.95, 42, 1521) = 0.67$$

The null–hypothesis was rejected. So the volatility was significantly higher in days with high news flow intensity. The results is given in Table 6.6 for several other companies .

So the volatility was significantly higher in days with high news flow intensity.

For most of the companies the variance levels in the marked days are significantly higher then in the not marked days (Figure 6.7). Stock return jumps were also seen on the days when extremely huge number of news arrived to the market. But the effect of the news number on the volatility is for a short term. For the days that follow the days with high news levels variance levels for marked and not marked days are the same (the required hypothesis was tested).

Table 6.6: Variance Comparison Tests Results

Company	Std. dev. for control group	Std. dev. for marked group	DF_1	DF_2	F
GB/ABF	0.0002	0.0140	-0.165	7.795	0.359
GB/BARC	-0.0004	0.0380	1.633	39.72	0.168
GB/BATS	0.0006	0.0150	0.174	12.017	0.356
GB/LLOY	-0.0010	0.0400	-1.039	33.394	0.154
GB/MKS	0.0001	0.0210	-1.851	28.816	0.146
GB/RDSA	0.0002	0.0180	0.339	9.824	0.710
GB/RR.	0.0006	0.0210	0.000	6.874	0.548

Note that this result is not a coincidence. The standard test does not detect difference in volatility in days before or follow the marked days. If we mark the days preceding the outliers in news intensity, the hypothesis of homogeneity of variances taken 59 cases out of 92. The day after outliers hypothesis not rejected in 35 cases out of 92.

Thus, it can be argued that during high-intensity news flow volatility was above average. Perhaps it can explain the volatility jumps.

Analysis of the market data for several companies allows to consider some additional aspects for the 2 component (smooth and jumps) volatility representation.

Firstly, we will investigate relative time evolution of smooth and jump-like volatility components for different companies.

Secondly, we will investigate whether regular and jump volatility are correlated or not. It is obvious that smooth component changes over time (ARCH effects are present). It is interesting to see whether jump component also has such behavioural patterns. We considere two extreme cases: jump-like volatility does not depend on the regular volatility component; jump-like volatility is 100% correlated with the regular volatility component. Thirdly, we are going to investigate whether the news effect on the stock prices is long-term or not. To explore this proposition, we will test, whether there is high volatility only in the days with

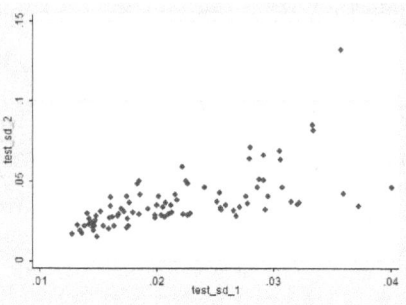

Figure 6.7: St. Dev. for labeled day and control groups

the high news intensity, or there are also such volatility effect in the previous and past days also. If this effect of the news intensity on the volatility propagates in the time, this would contradict the hypothesis of smooth and jump-like volatility components.

It is also interesting to investigate whether volatility jumps depend on the news intensity in particular day.

Let us consider the following simplified data generation process. We will divide our data into 2 groups.

In ordinary days variable J_t is equal to 0 and data could be generated as independent identically distributed variables with density with zero mean and variance σ_R^2.

$$r_t = R_t, R_t \sim iid(0, \sigma_R^2).$$

In the second data group $J_t = 1$ and our data could be represented as a sum of two random variables (regular component and jump)

$$r_t = R_t + V_t, R_t \sim iid(0, \sigma_R^2), V_t \sim iid(0, \sigma_J^2).$$

Consider the following relations for the expected value of observed values r_t^2. Assume that correlation coefficient of R and V is equal to ρ. First case: jump and regular component are independent. For the first group of data we will get

$$E(r_t^2|J_t = 0) = \sigma_R^2$$

while for the second

$$E(r_t^2|J_t = 1) = \sigma_R^2 + \sigma_J^2.$$

or, written in another form

$$E(r_t^2|J_t) = \sigma_R^2 + \sigma_J^2 J_t.$$

The last equation could be treated as regression model. Adding an error term, we get a standard regression model

$$r_t^2 = \sigma_R^2 + \sigma_J^2 J_t + u_t$$

or

$$r_t^2 = \beta_0 + \beta_1 J_t + u_t.$$

If we are to analyze data for several companies, we could write this model in the form of panel regression

$$r_{it}^2 = \beta_{0i} + \beta_{1i} J_{it} + u_{it},$$

where $i = 1, .., N$ is a company's number, β_{0i} - effect of the regular component, β_{1i} - effect of jumps. This notation brings certain advantages: it is easy to expand the model and there are standard procedures for hypothesis testing. For example, if hypothesis $H_0 : \beta_{11} = \beta_{12} = \ldots = \beta_{1N} = \beta_1$ (variance of jumps for all firms is the same) is true, our model will take the form

$$r_{it}^2 = \beta_{0i} + \beta_1 J_{it} + u_{it}.$$

To test this hypothesis we could employ a standard F-test. It is also possible to propose a model under assumption that variance of the jumps and regular component are on the same level. Dividing our initial equation

$$r_{it}^2 = \sigma_{Ri}^2 + \sigma_{Ji}^2 J_{it} + u_{it}$$

by the variance of the regular component s_{Ri}^2, we get

$$r_{it}^2/s_{Ri}^2 = 1 + \sigma_{Ji}^2/s_{Ri}^2 J_{it} + v_{it},$$

or

$$r_{it}^2/\sigma_{Ri}^2 = \beta_{0i} + \beta_{1i} J_{it} + v_{it}.$$

Hypothesis for our assumption will take the form

$$H_0 : \beta_{01} = \beta_{02} = \ldots = \beta_{0N} = 1; \beta_{10} = \beta_{12} = \ldots = \beta_{1N}$$

If we assume that variance of jumps is a linear function of some exogenous variable (for example, of the number of the news items N_{it},), then we could write our model as

$$r_{it}^2 = \beta_{0i} + \beta_1 J_{it} N_{it} + u_{it}.$$

Hereafter we will give estimation results for some of these models. Finally, the model under consideration allows for autoregressive processes. Such dynamic models will be treated in the chapters devoted to stochastic volatility. Consider also the case when jumps and regular components are fully correlated ($\rho = 1$). In this case

$$E(r_t^2 | J_t = 0) = \sigma_R^2,$$
$$E(r_t^2 | J_t = 1) = (\sigma_R + \sigma_J)^2 = \sigma_R^2(1 + \sigma_J/\sigma_R)^2 = \sigma_R^2(1 + \sigma_J/\sigma_R)^2 = \sigma_R^2 \delta.$$

Combining both equations, we get

$$E(r_t^2 | J_t) = \sigma_R^2 \delta^{J_t},$$

and, applying logarithmic transformation for both sides and introducing error term, we get the regression model

$$log(r_t^2) = \beta_0 + \beta_1 J_t + u_{it}.$$

In the case of several firms we will use panel data notation

$$log(r_{it}^2) = \beta_{0i} + \beta_{1i} J_{it} + u_{it}.$$

Consider that unconditional volatility in unlabeled days σ_U^2 is equal to regular volatility) $\sigma_U^2 = \sigma_R^2$, and volatility in labeled days σ_L^2 is equal the sum of regular and jump components $\sigma_L^2 = \sigma_R^2 + \sigma_J^2$, where σ^2 - unconditional volatility for stocks i at day t; σ_R^2 - regular volatility for stocks i at day t; σ_J^2 - jump variance stocks i at day t;

We use Hausman test with the null hypothesis as that the preferred model is random effects vs. the alternative the fixed effects. Because reported value of Chi-square is significant, we conclude that random effects is not appropriate and choose fixed effect estimators:

$$log(s_{it}^2) = \alpha_i + 0.47 J_{it}.$$

The elasticity volatility on dummy variables for jumps is equal 0.47. Therefore, the volatility in the days with at least one news is 1.5 times higher than that in other days.

Consider how quickly faded effect of volatility shock in time. Let $J_{it}^P = J_{it-1}$, $J_{it}^N = J_{it+1}$ be dummy variables. We consider the following model:

$$\log(r_{it}^2) = \alpha_i + \beta_1 J_{it}^P + \beta_2 J_{it} + \beta_3 J_{it}^N + \varepsilon_{it}$$

and obtain the estimation results:

$$\log(s_{it}^2) = \alpha_i + 0.19 J_{it}^P + 0.45 J_{it} + 0.12 J_{it}^N$$

Although the coefficients on the dummy variables for the previous and next days are significant, they are relatively small. Effect of news shocks is short-lived. It could be explained by the fact that arriving times and trading sessions do not coincide. The news arrive continuously, while the the trading session is limited in time, so errors may occur.

Positive news occur more often than negative ones in our data set. In addition it is possible that the market reacts differently to positive and negative news. Therefore, we include in the modelling number of positive and negative news:

$$\log(r_{it}^2) = \alpha_i + \beta_1 J_{it} + (\beta_2 E_{it}^- + \beta_3 E_{it}^+) J_{it} + \varepsilon_{it},$$

$$\log(r_{it}^2) = \alpha_i + \beta_1 J_{it} + (\beta_4 R_{it}^- + \beta_5 R_{it}^+) J_{it} + \varepsilon_{it},$$

where $E_{it}^-, E_{it}^+, R_{it}^-, R_{it}^+$ are logarithms of numbers negative (positive) event news and logarithms of numbers of negative (positive) relevant news for day t.

The estimation result indicates that there is no difference between coefficients for negative and positive event news. But the number of negative relevant news has little influence on volatility than the number of positive news:

$$\log(s_{it}^2) = \alpha_i + 0.28 J_{it} + (0.33 E_{it}^- + 0.39 E_{it}^+) J_{it},$$

$$\log(s_{it}^2) = \alpha_i + 0.28 J_{it} + (0.38 R_{it}^- + 0.17 R_{it}^+) J_{it}.$$

This result allows us to suggest that the news information can be useful for predicting not only jump days but also the size of the volatility jumps.

Let us compare this results with other method of labeling days with high news intensity. If day is marked when the relative number of news is bigger than certain threshold level c, i.e. $N_{it}/\sum_t N_{it} > c$, then the estimated equation for additive model is

$$\log(r_{it}^2) = \alpha_i + 0.68 J_{it}.$$

For multiplicative model we have

$$\log(s_{it}^2) = \alpha_i + 0.17 J_{it}^P + 0.65 J_{it} + 0.14 J_{it}^N.$$

that there is no long-lived impact of jumps to volatility.

Also the impact of the number of negative relevant news on volatility is more significant then impact of positive ones. It follows from equation

$$\log(s_{it}^2) = \alpha_i - 0.22 J_{it} + (0.44 R_{it}^- + 0.34 R_{it}^+) J_{it}.$$

Estimation results presented in this sections let us to conclude that time jumps may be predicted on the basis news information. Nevertheless, we do not take into account the dynamic nature of volatility process. In the next section we will apply stochastic volatility approach.

Chapter 7

Augmented GARCH Models

7.1 Augmented GARCH Models

7.1.1 Description of the Models

Recent studies on the volatility of stock returns have been dominated by time series models of conditional heteroscedasticity and have found strong support for ARCH-GARCH-type effects. However, ARCH-GARCH-type models do not provide a theoretical explanation of volatility or what, if any, the exact contributions of information flows are in the volatility-generating process. One theoretical explanation is the mixture of distribution hypothesis (MDH) advanced by Clark [1973], Epps and Epps [1976], Tauchen and Pitts [1983], and Lamoureax and Lastrapes [1991]. The MDH argues that the variance of returns at a given interval is proportional to the rate of information arrival. As a result, volatility clustering could be a reflection of the serial correlation of information arrival frequencies. All traders simultaneously receive the new price signals and the shift to a new equilibrium is immediate and there will be no intermediate partial equilibrium.

The MDH relies on the following assumptions:

- returns and corresponding trade volumes are jointly independently distributed with finite variance (Harris [1987]);

- the number of events occurring each day is stochastic.

Some of empirical studies, including a pioneer work for the US stock market by Lamoureax and Lastrapes [1990], have found evidence that the inclusion of trading volumes in GARCH models for returns results in a decrease of the estimated persistence, or even causes it to disappear. However, the results from other research indicated that trading volume contributes some information to the returns process, while their results also show persistence in volatility even after incorporate volume effects. These research paper include the futures market by Najand and Yung in Najand and Yung [1991].

If the parameters α, β of GARCH(1,1) model are positive, then shocks to volatility persist over time. The sum $\alpha + \beta$ of these parameters reflects the degree of persistence. Denote by δ_{it} the ith intraday equilibrium price increment in day t. Lamoureux and Lastrapes Lamoureax and Lastrapes [1990] suggest that the innovation upon stock returns is a linear combination of intraday price movements, i.e.,

$$\epsilon_t = \sum_{i=1}^{n_t} \delta_{it},$$

n_t is the number of information flows within day t. Thus, Lamoureux and Lastrapes (Lamoureax and Lastrapes [1990]) consider $\epsilon_t = r_t - \mu_{t-1}$ as an aggregation of price innovations from information flows into the market. Note that they do not differentiate on the type of information flows into the market.

Assume δ_{it} is independent identically distributed with mean zero and variance σ^2 and suppose that n_t is large. Then it follows from the central limit theorem that $\epsilon_t | n_t$ is asymptotically distributed as $\mathcal{N}(0, \sigma^2 n_t)$. Then

$$\Omega_t := \mathbb{E}(\epsilon_t^2 | n_t) = \sigma^2 n_t. \tag{7.1}$$

Suppose that n_t's are serially correlated:

$$n_t = a + b(L)n_{t-1} + u_t, \tag{7.2}$$

where a is a constant, $b(L)$ is a lag polynomial of order q, i.e. $b(L)n_{t-1} = \sum_{k=1}^{q} b_k n_{t-k}$, u_t is a white noise.

Substituting representation (7.2) into equation (7.1), we get

$$\Omega_t = \sigma^2 a + b(L)\Omega_{t-1} + \sigma^2 u_t. \tag{7.3}$$

Equation (7.3) describes the conditional variance of returns is depends on lagged conditional variances and a white noise term. It motivated Lamoureax and Lastrapes [1990] to use additive GARCH-Volume model. As it was mentioned by Lamoureux and Lastrapes Lamoureax and Lastrapes [1990], equation (7.3) captures GARCH-type persistence in conditional variance. However, in the paper (Bauer and Nieuwland [1995]) it was pointed out that the link between (7.3) and GARCH model is not at all straightforward.

The question is what is the best proxy for n_t?

Trading volume can be a good proxies for news arrivals. It follows from the intuitive fact that the more company news arrives, the more investors will interpret the impact of the news differently, and thus the more investors will have an impetus to trade as their expectations about future returns differ.

Lamoureux and Lastrapes (Lamoureax and Lastrapes [1990]) suppose that volume can be considered as a proportional proxy for information arrivals to the market. Volume acts as a mixing variable, i.e. ϵ_t is assumed to be random draws upon alternative distributions, with variances depending upon information available at the time. It leads to a model (7.4), (7.5), where V_t is the volume of trade that occurs in time t.

Following the studies by previous authors, we are trying to estimate four alternative augmented GARCH models of volatility.

We will examine the following alternative GARCH models:

1. *GARCH model augmented with volume.*

   We will consider a process (ϵ_t) such that

   $$\epsilon_t = \sigma_t u_t, t \in \mathbb{Z}, \tag{7.4}$$

where (σ_t) is a nonnegative process such that

$$\sigma_t^2 = \omega + \alpha\epsilon_{t-1}^2 + \beta\sigma_{t-1}^2 + \gamma V_t, \tag{7.5}$$

where $V_t = v_t/v^*$ is the scaled trade volume of the stock at the day t (v_t is daily trade volume of the stock at the day t and $v^* = \max_t v_t$), $\omega > 0$, $\alpha, \beta \geq 0$, $\alpha + \beta < 1$ and γ are parameters of the model.

2. *GARCH model augmented with lagged volume.*

   We will consider a process (ϵ_t) such that

   $$\epsilon_t = \sigma_t u_t, t \in \mathbb{Z}, \tag{7.6}$$

   where (σ_t) is a nonnegative process such that

   $$\sigma_t^2 = \omega + \alpha\epsilon_{t-1}^2 + \beta\sigma_{t-1}^2 + \gamma V_{t-1}, \tag{7.7}$$

   where V_{t-1} is the scaled trade volume for the company in day $t - 1$, $\omega > 0$, $\alpha, \beta \geq 0$, $\alpha + \beta < 1$ and γ are parameters of the model.

3. *GARCH model augmented with news intensity.*

   Let r_t and r_t^* denote the log return of the company and log return of FTSE100 index at interval t respectively. We will consider a process $(\epsilon_t) = r_t - (\theta_1 + \theta_2 r_t^*)$ such that

   $$\epsilon_t = \sigma_t u_t, t \in \mathbb{Z}, \tag{7.8}$$

   where (σ_t) is a nonnegative process such that

   $$\sigma_t^2 = \omega + \alpha\epsilon_{t-1}^2 + \beta\sigma_{t-1}^2 + \gamma n_t, \tag{7.9}$$

   where n_t is the number of all relevant news for the company released at the day t, $\omega > 0$, $\alpha, \beta \geq 0$, $\alpha + \beta < 1$, γ, θ_1 and θ_2 are parameters of the model.

4. *GARCH model augmented with lagged news intensity.*

   Let r_t and r_t^* denote the log return of the company and log return of FTSE100 index at interval t respectively. We will consider a process $(\epsilon_t) = r_t - (\theta_1 + \theta_2 r_t^*)$ such that

   $$\epsilon_t = \sigma_t u_t, t \in \mathbb{Z}, \tag{7.10}$$

   where (σ_t) is a nonnegative process such that

   $$\sigma_t^2 = \omega + \alpha\epsilon_{t-1}^2 + \beta\sigma_{t-1}^2 + \gamma n_{t-1}, \tag{7.11}$$

where n_{t-1} is the number of all relevant news for the company released at the day $t - 1$, $\omega > 0$, $\alpha, \beta \geq 0$, $\alpha + \beta < 1$, γ, θ_1 and θ_2 are parameters of the model.

The first model is the model with contemporaneous trade volume. The second model is the model with lagged trade volume. The third model is the models with contemporaneous news intensity and the forth is with lagged news intensity. The number of news about a company at the day t is called the news intensity at the day t.

Empirical results can be found in the section 7.2. It will be shown that

- the GARCH(1,1) model augmented with volume V_t removes GARCH and ARCH effects for most of the FTSE100 companies.

- the GARCH(1,1) model augmented with lagged volume V_{t-1} does not remove GARCH and ARCH effects.

- the GARCH(1,1) model augmented with the news intensity n_t does not necessary remove GARCH and ARCH effects; however, using likelihood ratio test it will be shown that the model performs better than both the "pure" GARCH model for most of the FTSE100 companies.

- the GARCH(1,1) model augmented with the *lagged* news intensity n_{t-1} does not remove GARCH and ARCH effects.

7.1.2 Maximum likelihood estimation of augmented GARCH models

To calibrate the GARCH$(1, 1)$ model we can use different methods including the least-square estimator or generalized moment method, but in this work we will apply the maximum likelihood approach.

One can generalized models (7.4)–(7.5), (7.10)–(7.11), (7.8)–(7.9) in the following way.

Let (ϵ_t) be a process such that

$$\epsilon_t = \sigma_t u_t, t \in \mathbb{Z}, \tag{7.12}$$

where (σ_t) is a nonnegative process such that

$$\sigma_t^2 = \omega + \alpha \epsilon_{t-1}^2 + \beta_1 \sigma_{t-1}^2 + f(s_t, \mu), \tag{7.13}$$

where s_t is an exogenous time series, $f(\cdot, \mu) : \mathbb{R} \to \mathbb{R}$ is a continuous function with a vector of parameters μ, $\omega > 0$, $\alpha, \beta \geq 0$, $\alpha + \beta < 1$ and μ are parameters of the model.

The subsection describes quasi-maximum likelihood estimation (QML) of model (7.12), (7.13)

The vector of model parameters is

$$\theta = (\omega, \alpha, \beta, \mu)^T.$$

We will assume that θ belongs to the set

$$\Theta := \{(\omega, \alpha, \beta, \mu)^T : \omega > 0, \alpha > 0, \beta > 0 \in \mathbb{R}\}.$$

Denote

$$\theta^* = (\omega^*, \alpha^*, \beta^*, \mu^*)^T$$

the vector of the true values of parameters. The aim is to find θ^* that maximize a QML function given an observation sequence

$$\epsilon_0, \ldots, \epsilon_n$$

of length n.

Define the sequence $(\tilde{\sigma}_1, \ldots, \tilde{\sigma}_n)$ by recursion:

$$\tilde{\sigma}_t^2 = \omega + \alpha \epsilon_{t-1}^2 + \beta \tilde{\sigma}_{t-1}^2 + f(s_t, \mu), \ 1 \leq t \leq n,$$

where ϵ_0 and $\tilde{\sigma}_0$ are an initial values of ϵ's and σ's respectively.

Given the initial values, the Gaussian quasi-likelihood function can be written as follows

$$L_n(\theta) = L_n(\theta; \epsilon_1, \ldots, \epsilon_n) = \prod_{t=1}^{n} \frac{1}{\sqrt{2\pi\tilde{\sigma}_t^2}} \exp\left(-\frac{\epsilon_t^2}{2\tilde{\sigma}_t^2}\right)$$

The optimal estimation of θ is defined by

$$\tilde{\theta} = \arg \max_{\theta \in \Theta} L_n(\theta) = \arg \max_{\theta \in \Theta} F_n(\theta),$$

where

$$F_n(\theta) := - \sum_{t=1}^{n} \left(\frac{\epsilon_t^2}{\tilde{\sigma}_t^2} + \log \tilde{\sigma}_t^2 \right)$$

is log quasi-likelihood function (constant terms are ignored).

7.2   Empirical Study

7.2.1   GARCH(1,1) Model with Volume

The aim of this section is to examine the impact of trading volume using GARCH approach suggested by Lamoureax and Lastrapes [1990].

1. Data description

Our sample covers a period ranging from July 5, 2005 to July 5, 2008 (i.e. 750 trading days). Our sample is composed of the 92 UK stocks that were part of the FTSE100 index in the beginning of 2005 and which survived through the period of 6 years. We have deleted 8 stocks. In this work we will present empirical results of only 5 company from the FTSE100. We focus our attention only on five companies traded on London Stock Exchange: AVIVA plc, BP, BT Group plc, Lloyd Banking Group, HSBC HLDG.

Daily stock closing prices (the last daily transaction price of the security), as well as daily transactions volume (number of shares traded during the day) are obtained from Yahoo Finance database. Results similar to one's presented in the chapter can be verified for all FTSE100 companies.

Table 7.1 provides preliminary descriptive statistics for the stock prices log returns and trading volumes.

Table 7.1: Descriptive statistics of five companies traded on London Stock Exchange

Company	T	Period	Mean	Std.Dev.	Skew.	Kurt.	Vol.Mean
Aviva	750	05/06/2005-05/06/2008	0.0001	0.0135	-0.3142	4.6735	1.12E+07
BP	750	05/06/2005-05/06/2008	0.0003	0.0121	0.0252	3.4093	7.76E+07
BT GROUP	750	05/06/2005-05/06/2008	0.0004	0.0134	0.4950	6.1042	4.46E+07
Lloyds	750	05/06/2005-05/06/2008	0.0000	0.0121	-0.2210	6.7680	3.26E+07
HSBC	750	05/06/2005-05/06/2008	-0.0001	0.0089	-0.0854	5.0921	4.13E+07

Table 7.2 presents

- the list of stocks,

- the Kiefer-Salmon skewness test statistic (S)

- the Kiefer-Salmon kurtosis statistic (K)

- the Kiefer-Salmon joint statistic for normality (S+K)

- p-value of the Shapiro-Wilk statistic (marginal significance level)

- the Box-Ljung Q-statistic, constructed for maximum lag of 20.

It is well-known that S and K are $\chi^2(1)$-distributed, and $K + S$ is $\chi^2(2)$-distributed.

Based on the results presented in Table 7.2 one can conclude that the null hypothesis of normality is rejected for all stocks but BP.

The Box-Ljung Q-statistic tests for serial correlation in the daily volume series. It shows that there is no autocorrelation of log returns.

Table 7.2: Empirical properties of daily log returns and volumes for the five stocks in the sample

Company	S	K	SW(p)	Q(20)
AVIVA	0.0005	0.0000	0.9778	1292.7818
BP	0.7759	0.0376	0.9969	1730.2602
BT GROUP	0.0000	0.0000	0.9667	549.1024
Lloyds	0.0135	0.0000	0.9489	939.2284
HSBC	0.3361	0.0000	0.9746	1942.3059

Consistent with the findings in Lamoureux and Lastrapes Lamoureax and Lastrapes [1990], we find that the p-values of Shapiro-Wilk statistic of log returns for all five companies are close to zero. We may conclude that all series are non-normal.

2. Empirical results

The GARCH model of Bollerslev [1986] provides a flexible and parsimonious approximation to conditional variance dynamics. Maximum likelihood estimates of "pure" GARCH(1,1) model (without Volume) for log returns of closing daily prices are presented in Table 7.3. Using GARCH estimates, Table 7.3 shows that the coefficients of the model are highly significant and volatility persistence, i.e. $\alpha + \beta$, is more than 0.9. It provides clear evidence of GARCH effect.

Table 7.3: Maximum likelihood estimates of "pure" GARCH(1,1) model (without Volume) for log returns of closing daily prices, $\sigma_t^2 = \omega + \alpha \epsilon_{t-1}^2 + \beta \sigma_{t-1}^2$

Company	α	β	$\alpha + \beta$	LLF_1
AVIVA	0.1209	0.8549	0.9758	2794.08
BP	0.0515	0.9208	0.9723	2867.78
BT GROUP	0.0770	0.8683	0.9454	2786.33
Lloyd	0.1230	0.8609	0.9839	2874.06
HSBC	0.1232	0.8568	0.9800	3112.39

The estimates of GARCH model with volume (7.4), (7.5) are presented in Table

7.4. The results show us that daily trading volume has significant explanatory power regarding the conditional volatility of daily log return for 3 of 5 companies (AVIVA, BP and BT Group). For Lloyds Group and HSBC Group there are not any changes in the level of persistence $\alpha + \beta$ compare to the results for the "pure" GARCH model.

The same contradictory picture is held for other FTSE100 companies. Once volume V_t is included as an explanatory variable in the equation, for many of FTSE100 companies the sum of $\alpha + \beta$ is significantly less than corresponding results in Table 7.3. One can see that once contemporaneous volume is included as an exogenous variable in the model, the impact of log return on volatility diminishes for most of FTSE100 companies.

Table 7.4: Maximum likelihood estimates of GARCH(1,1) model with Volume for log returns of the closing daily prices, $\sigma_t^2 = \omega + \alpha \epsilon_{t-1}^2 + \beta \sigma_{t-1}^2 + \gamma V_t$

Company	α	β	γ	$\alpha + \beta$	LLF_2
AVIVA	0.2309	0.0012	1.22E-03	0.2321	2794.92
BP	0.1617	0.0000	7.19E-04	0.1617	2875.73
BT GROUP	0.1618	0.0000	9.38E-04	0.1618	2862.26
Lloyds	0.0928	0.8573	7.97E-05	0.9501	2883.04
HSBC	0.1387	0.8065	2.58E-05	0.9453	3118.81

Let us remind that $V_t = v_t/v^*$, where v_t is daily trade volume of a stock at the day t and $v^* = \max_t v_t$.

The estimates of γ in Table 7.4 for all five stocks are comparable with the square of unconditional standard deviation of the stocks (see Table 7.1).

To estimate the impact of lagged volume on volatility persistence in GARCH model, we consider a nonnegative process $\epsilon_t = \sigma_t u_t$, such that

$$\sigma_t = \omega + \alpha \epsilon_{t-1}^2 + \beta_1 \sigma_{t-1} + \gamma V_{t-1}, \qquad (7.14)$$

where V_{t-1} is the scaled trade volume for the company in day $t-1$, $\omega > 0$, $\alpha, \beta \geq 0$, $\alpha + \beta < 1$ and γ are parameters of the model.

The results presented in Table 7.9 show that there are no evidence of vanishing effect of log return on volatility. Moreover, estimates of parameters α, β are close to corresponding ones in Table 7.3.

Table 7.5: Maximum likelihood estimates of GARCH(1,1) model with *Lagged* Volume for log returns of the closing daily prices, $\sigma_t^2 = \omega + \alpha\epsilon_{t-1}^2 + \beta\sigma_{t-1}^2 + \gamma V_{t-1}$

Company	α	β	γ	$\alpha + \beta$	LLF_3
AVIVA	0.1150	0.8683	3.55E-05	0.9832	2794.78
BP	0.0516	0.9208	3.41E-11	0.9723	2867.78
BT GROUP	0.0761	0.8803	2.40E-11	0.9564	2867.22
Lloyds	0.0514	0.9208	3.32E-11	0.9721	2790.64
HSBC	0.1181	0.8574	1.20E-05	0.9755	3113.12

Note that the GARCH model (the null model) is a special case of the GARCH model augmented with volume (the alternative model). Therefore, to compare the fit of two models it can be used a likelihood ratio test (see e.g. Cox and Hinkley [1974]). It is the most common approach to testing problem. The test was introduced by Neyman and Pearson in 1928. It compares the maximum likelihood under the alternatives with that under the hypothesis. Let us remind the main idea of the test. Let the likelihood function of θ is

$$LF(x, \theta) = p_\theta(x),$$

i.e. the probability density (or probability) of x considered as a function of θ. It is widely considered a (relative) measure of support that the observation x gives to the parameter θ. Then the likelihood ratio compares the best explanation the data provide for the alternatives with the best explanations for the hypothesis. The likelihood ratio is a function of the data x, therefore it is a statistic. The likelihood-ratio test rejects the null hypothesis if the value of this statistic is too small. We must compare the value of likelihood ratio to a critical value to decide whether to reject the null model in favor of the alternative model.

Results of likelihood ratio test for GARCH model (null model) and GARCH model augmented with volume (alternative model) one can find in Table 7.6. For four of five companies the alternative model is preferable with confidence level of 1%.

Results of likelihood ratio test for GARCH model (null model) and GARCH model augmented with *lagged* volume (alternative model) one can find in Table

Table 7.6: Results of the likelihood ratio test for GARCH model and GARCH model augmented with volume

Company	LLF_1	LLF_2	$2(LLF_2 - LLF_1)$	$\chi^2(1), 1\%$	Null Hyp.
AVIVA	2794.08	2794.92	1.70	6.64	accepted
BP	2867.78	2875.73	15.89	6.64	rejected
BT Group	2786.33	2862.26	151.87	6.64	rejected
Lloyds	2874.06	2883.04	17.96	6.64	rejected
HSBC	3112.39	3118.81	12.84	6.64	rejected

7.7. For four of five companies the alternative model is rejected with confidence level of 1%.

Table 7.7: Results of the likelihood ratio test for GARCH model and GARCH model augmented with *lagged* volume

Company	LLF_1	LLF_3	$2(LLF_3 - LLF_1)$	$\chi^2(1), 1\%$	Null Hyp.
AVIVA	2794.08	2794.78	1.42	6.64	accepted
BP	2867.78	2867.78	0.00	6.64	accepted
BT Group	2786.33	2790.64	8.63	6.64	rejected
Lloyds	2874.06	2874.64	1.15	6.64	accepted
HSBC	3112.39	3113.12	1.45	6.64	accepted

Figure 7.1 presents the volatility forecast of GARCH model and GARCH model with Volume for HSBC stock market closing daily prices.

7.2.2   GARCH(1,1) Model Augmented with News Intensity

1. Data Description

Our sample covers a period ranging from July 5, 2005 to July 5, 2008 (i.e. 750 trading days). Our sample is composed of the 92 UK stocks that were part of the FTSE100 index in the beginning of 2005 and which survived through the period of 6 years. We have deleted 8 stocks. In this work we will present empirical results

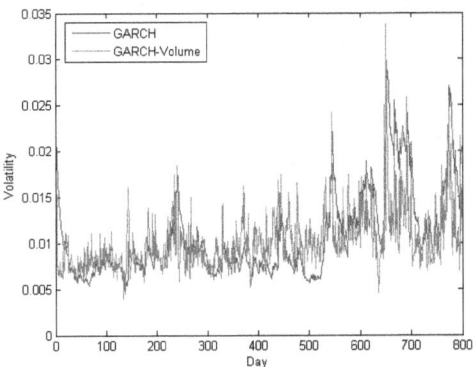

Figure 7.1: Volatility forecast of GARCH model and GARCH model with Volume for HSBC stock market closing daily prices (05/06/2005-05/06/2008)

of only 5 company from the FTSE100. We focus our attention only on five companies traded on London Stock Exchange: AVIVA, BP, BT Group, Lloyd Banking Group, HSBC. Daily stock closing prices (the last daily transaction price of the security) are obtained from Yahoo Finance database. Table 7.1 provides preliminary descriptive statistics for the stock prices log returns and trading volumes.

All news analytics data were given by Raven Pack News Analytics (RPNA). RPNA is a news sentiment analysis service that provides a look into the sentiment of more than 28,000 publicly traded companies worldwide. Each score is a weighed balance of sentiment in articles published by professional newswires (such as Dow Jones and Reuters) and hundreds of financial sites, online newspapers and even blogs.

For each news wire, we have got the following fields (Table 6.1): time stamp, company name, company id, relevance of the news, event category, event sentiment, novelty of the news, novelty id, composite sentiment score of the news, word/phrase level score, projections by company, editorials & commentary, reports corp actions, news impact projection, story ID. Company, relevance score, composite sentiment score are the main fields of interest. One piece of news can of course concern several companies, industries and subjects. To avoid any redundancy and duplicate announcements that do not bring any additional information value, we restrict the sample to news released with high relevance score (more or equal to 90). We do not eliminate all news releases with the same headlines and lead paragraphs, since it is supposed that the number of the same news published by different news agencies reflects the importance of the news.

For example, there was more than 8000 financial BP news releases with relevance ≥ 90 over the whole sample period.

Figure 7.2 shows the evolution over time of the total daily number of news wires for BP company.

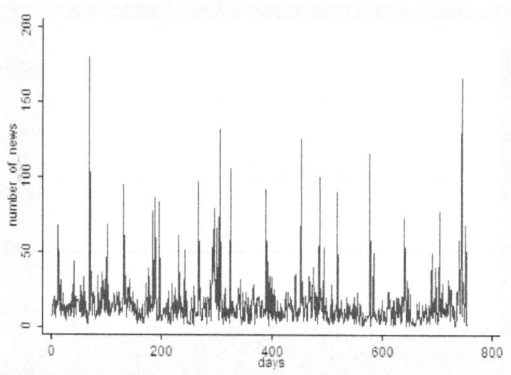

Figure 7.2: The dynamics of British Petroleum' news announcements

Figure 7.3 displays the evolution over time of the rolling mean of the number of news wires with 5-days window.

One can see that there is no any clear trend both in Figure 7.2 and Figure 7.3. It could indicate that the news time-series is rather stationary and reduce the risk of dummy results due to a possible simultaneous increase over time of the

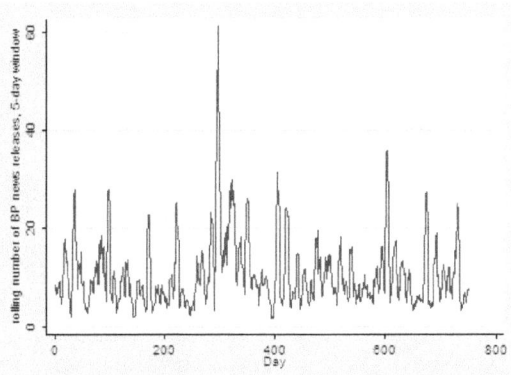

Figure 7.3: The rolling mean of the number of British Petroleum' news announcements, 5-days window (January 3, 2005 – December 31, 2007)

stock volatility. Some periods have rate of news intensity below the average (e.g. holidays, Christmas time). On the other hand, one can witnessed the increase of the rate at the periods of the quarterly reports and releases of the intermediate figures and earnings of companies.

One can see a clear presence of weekly seasonality in the data. For example, Figure 7.4 shows that the average number of British Petroleum' news announcements released during the week-end is much lower than the one of the other weekdays. The same picture is held for all FTSE100 companies indeed. Since that we exclude all weekend news from our analysis.

Figure 7.5 shows the evolution of the frequency of announcements arrivals throughout the day (at New-York's time) for BP company. There are picks at 9 am and 4 pm, and the activity seems to be globally more sustained in the morning than in the afternoon. The "lunch drop" is easily recognizable.

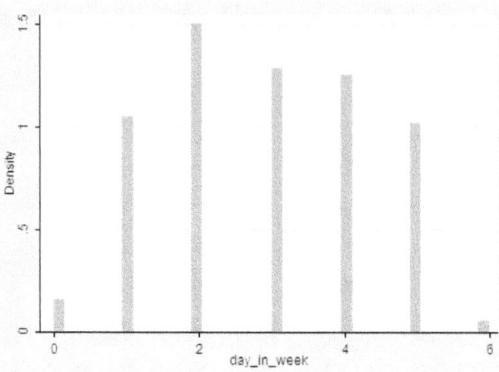

Figure 7.4: The average number of British Petroleum' news announcements released per day in week

2. Empirical Results

The estimates of GARCH model with news intensity (7.8), (7.9) are presented in Table 7.8. The results show us that daily news intensity has some explanatory power regarding the conditional volatility of daily log return. Once news intensity n_t is included as an explanatory variable in the equation, the sum of $\alpha + \beta$ is less than corresponding results in Table 7.3. One can see that once contemporaneous news intensity is included as an exogenous variable in the model, the GARCH effect slightly diminishes for some companies (BP and HSBC Group).

To estimate the impact of lagged news intensity on volatility persistence in GARCH model, we consider a nonnegative process $\epsilon_t = \sigma_t u_t$, such that

$$\sigma_t^2 = \omega + \alpha \epsilon_{t-1}^2 + \beta_1 \sigma_{t-1}^2 + \gamma n_{t-1}, \tag{7.15}$$

where n_{t-1} is the news intensity for the company in day $t-1$, $\omega > 0$, $\alpha, \beta \geq 0$, $\alpha + \beta < 1$ and γ are parameters of the model.

The results presented in Table 7.9 show that there are no evidence of vanishing

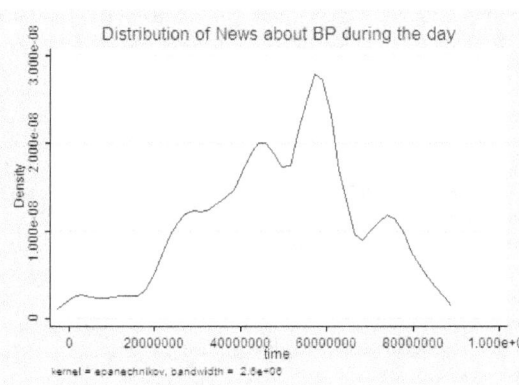

Figure 7.5: The average number of British Petroleum' news announcements released during the day

GARCH effect. Moreover, estimates of parameters α, β are close to corresponding ones in Table 7.3.

Results of likelihood ratio test for GARCH model (null model) and GARCH model augmented with news intensity (alternative model) one can find in Table 7.10. For all five companies the alternative model is preferable with confidence level of 1%.

Results of likelihood ratio test for GARCH model (null model) and GARCH model augmented with *lagged* news intensity (alternative model) one can find in Table 7.11. For all five companies the alternative model is rejected with confidence level of 1%.

Figure 7.6 presents the volatility forecast performed by GARCH model and GARCH model with Volume for HSBC stock market closing daily prices.

Table 7.8: Maximum likelihood estimates of GARCH(1,1) model with news intensity for log returns of the closing daily prices, $(\epsilon_t) = r_t - (\theta_1 + \theta_2 r_t^*)$, $\sigma_t^2 = \omega + \alpha \epsilon_{t-1}^2 + \beta \sigma_{t-1}^2 + \gamma n_t$

Company	α	β	γ	θ_1	θ_2	$\alpha + \beta$	LLF_4
AVIVA	0.0001	0.9562	2.24E-06	-4.36E-04	1.2086	0.9563	2963.51
BP	0.0010	0.1428	5.39E-06	-1.17E-04	0.9814	0.1437	3086.74
BT GROUP	0.0811	0.7595	8.36E-06	1.23E-05	0.7568	0.8406	2944.74
Lloyds	0.1500	0.8109	4.39E-06	7.38E-05	0.9655	0.9609	3134.81
HSBC	0.1448	0.1343	3.68E-06	-4.16E-04	0.8534	0.2791	3309.99

Table 7.9: Maximum likelihood estimates of GARCH(1,1) model with *Lagged* news intensity for log returns of the closing daily prices, $(\epsilon_t) = r_t - (\theta_1 + \theta_2 r_t^*)$, $\sigma_t^2 = \omega + \alpha \epsilon_{t-1}^2 + \beta \sigma_{t-1}^2 + \gamma n_{t-1}$

Company	α	β	γ	θ_1	θ_2	$\alpha + \beta$	LLF_5
AVIVA	0.1178	0.8076	5.80E-12	-5.51E-04	1.1715	0.9254	3039.36
BP	0.0199	0.9494	2.94E-13	1.25E-04	0.9325	0.9694	3113.03
BT GROUP	0.0863	0.7105	1.12E-20	1.43E-05	0.8129	0.7968	2907.11
Lloyds	0.1366	0.8380	1.76E-14	3.51E-05	0.9716	0.9746	3113.29
HSBC	0.1544	0.7830	3.08E-24	-1.14E-05	0.7704	0.9375	3306.47

3. Conclusion

The results show us that daily trading volume does have significant explanatory power regarding the conditional volatility of daily log return. Based on empirical study for stocks of some of FTSE100 companies we may conclude that once contemporaneous volume is included as an exogenous variable in the model, the GARCH effect diminishes for most of the FTSE100 companies.

However, the results presented in Table 7.9 show that there are no evidence of vanishing GARCH effect for the GARCH(1,1) model augmented with *lagged* volume V_{t-1}.

Then we merely reproduce the methodology commonly used in the literature (see Kalev et al. [2004] and Janssen [2004]). It sums up to insert the number of

Table 7.10: Results of the likelihood ratio test for GARCH model and GARCH model augmented with news intensity

Company	LLF_1	LLF_4	$2(LLF_4 - LLF_1)$	$\chi^2(3), 1\%$	Null Hyp.
AVIVA	2794.08	2963.51	338.88	7.82	rejected
BP	2867.78	3086.74	437.94	7.82	rejected
BT Group	2786.33	2944.74	316.83	7.82	rejected
Lloyds	2874.06	3134.81	521.51	7.82	rejected
HSBC	3112.39	3309.99	395.21	7.82	rejected

Table 7.11: Results of the likelihood ratio test for GARCH model and GARCH model augmented with *lagged* news intensity

Company	LLF_1	LLF_5	$2(LLF_5 - LLF_1)$	$\chi^2(3), 1\%$	Null Hyp.
AVIVA	2794.08	3039.36	490.57	7.82	rejected
BP	2867.78	3113.03	490.50	7.82	rejected
BT Group	2786.33	2907.11	241.57	7.82	rejected
Lloyds	2874.06	3113.29	478.46	7.82	rejected
HSBC	3112.39	3306.47	388.17	7.82	rejected

daily announcements concerning a stock into the equation of its variance in a GARCH (1,1) model. The estimation of the latter after inclusion of the variable NBN (daily number of news releases) converges for all 5 stocks. It was shown that the GARCH(1,1) model augmented with the news intensity n_t (the number of daily announcements) does not necessarily remove GARCH and ARCH effects.

However, the likelihood ratio test shows that the GARCH(1,1) model augmented with the news intensity performs better than both the GARCH model.

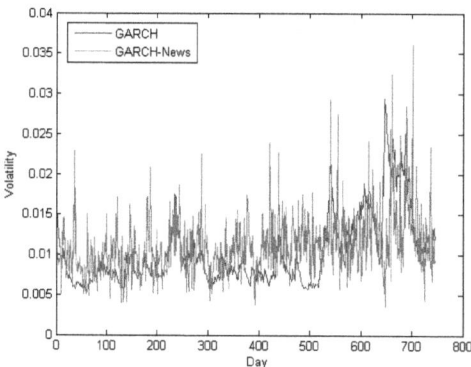

Figure 7.6: Volatility forecast by GARCH model and GARCH model with news
intensity for HSBC stock market closing daily prices (05/06/2005-05/06/2008)

Chapter 8

GARCH models with Jumps

8.1 GARCH model with Jumps

8.1.1 Model Description

GARCH-Jump model was proposed and studied in Maheu and McCurdy [2004]. This paper proposes a model of conditional variance of returns implied by the impact of different type of news.

Let X_t be the log return of a particular stock or the market portfolio from time $t-1$ to time t. Let I_{t-1} denotes the past information set containing the realized values of all relevant variables up to time $t-1$. Suppose investors know the information in I_{t-1} when they make their investment decision at time $t-1$. Then the relevant expected return μ_t to the investors is the conditional expected value of X_t, given I_{t-1}, i.e.

$$\mu_t = E(X_t|I_{t-1}).$$

The relevant expected volatility σ_t^2 to the investors is conditional variance of X_t, given I_{t-1}, i.e.

$$\sigma_t^2 = Var(X_t|I_{t-1}).$$

Then

$$\epsilon_t = X_t - \mu_t$$

is the unexpected return at time t.

In GARCH–Jump model it is supposed that news process have two separate components (normal and unusual news), which cause two types of innovation (smooth and jump-like innovations):

$$\epsilon_t = \epsilon_{1,t} + \epsilon_{2,t}. \tag{8.1}$$

These two news innovations have a different impact on return volatility. It is assumed that the first component $\epsilon_{1,t}$ reflects the impact of unobservable normal news innovations, while the second one $\epsilon_{2,t}$ is caused by unusual news events.

The first term in (8.1) reflects the impact of normal news to volatility:

$$\epsilon_{1,t} = \sigma_t u_t, t \in \mathbb{Z},$$

where (u_n) be a sequence of i.i.d. random variables such that $u_t \sim \mathcal{N}(0,1)$, (σ_t) is a nonnegative GARCH(1,1) process such that

$$\sigma_t^2 = \alpha_0 + \alpha_1 \epsilon_{t-1}^2 + \beta_1 \sigma_{t-1}^2$$

and $\alpha_0, \alpha_1, \beta_1 > 0$. Note that $\mathbb{E}(\epsilon_{1,t}|I_{t-1}) = 0$.

The second term in (8.1) is a jump innovation with $\mathbb{E}(\epsilon_{2,t}|I_{t-1}) = 0$. The component $\epsilon_{2,t}$ is a result of unexpected events and is responsible for jumps in volatility.

The distribution of jumps is assumed to be Poisson distribution. Let λ_t be intensity parameter of Poisson distribution. Denote n_t a number of jumps occurring between time $t - 1$ and t. Then conditional density of n_t is

$$P(n_t = j|I_{t-1}) = \frac{\exp(-\lambda_t)\lambda_t^j}{j!}, \ j = 0, 1, \ldots. \tag{8.2}$$

We suppose that the intensity parameter λ_t conditionally varies over time. It is assumed that the conditional jump intensity $\lambda_t = \mathbb{E}(n_t|I_{t-1})$, i.e. the expected number of jumps occurring between time $t - 1$ and t conditional on information I_{t-1}, has dynamics

$$\lambda_t = \lambda_0 + \rho\lambda_{t-1} + \gamma_1\zeta_{t-1}. \tag{8.3}$$

The process (8.3) is called an autoregressive conditional jump intensity and was proposed in the paper Chan and Maheu [2002]. The model based on the assumption that the conditional jump intensity is autoregressive and related both to the last period's conditional jump intensity and to an intensity residual ζ_{t-1}. The intensity residual ζ_{t-1} is defined as

$$\zeta_{t-1} = \mathbb{E}(n_{t-1}|I_{t-1}) - \lambda_{t-1} = \sum_{j=0}^{\infty} j P(n_{t-1} = j|I_{t-1}) - \lambda_{t-1}.$$

Here $\mathbb{E}(n_{t-1}|I_{t-1})$ is the expected number of jumps occurring from $t - 2$ to $t - 1$, and λ_{t-1} is the conditional expectation of numbers of jumps n_{t-1} given the information I_{t-2} available at the moment $t - 2$. Thus

$$\zeta_{t-1} = \mathbb{E}(n_{t-1}|I_{t-1}) - \mathbb{E}(n_{t-1}|I_{t-2})$$

i.e. ζ_{t-1} represents the change in the econometrician's conditional forecast of n_{t-1} as the information set is updated from $t-2$ to $t-1$. It is easy to see that $\mathbb{E}(\zeta_t|I_{t-1}) = 0$, i.e. ζ_t is a martingale difference sequence with respect to I_{t-1}, and therefore $\mathbb{E}(\zeta_t) = 0$, $\mathrm{Cov}(\zeta_t, \zeta_{t-i}) = 0$ for all $i > 0$.

Denote $Y_{t,k}$ the size of k-th jump that occur from time $t - 1$ to t, $1 \le k \le n_t$. In the model it is supposed that the jump size $Y_{t,k}$ is realization of normal distributed random:

$$Y_{t,k} \sim \mathcal{N}(\theta, \delta^2).$$

Then the cumulative jump size J_t from $t - 1$ to t is equal to the sum of all jumps occurring from time $t - 1$ to t:

$$J_t = \sum_{k=1}^{n_t} Y_{t,k}.$$

The jump innovation $\epsilon_{2,t}$ defined by

$$\epsilon_{2,t} = J_t - \mathbb{E}(J_t|I_{t-1}).$$

It follows from

$$\mathbb{E}(J_t|I_{t-1}) = \theta\lambda_t$$

that

$$\epsilon_{2,t} = \sum_{k=1}^{n_t} Y_{t,k} - \theta \lambda_t.$$

Therefore we have

$$\mathbb{E}(\epsilon_{2,t}|I_{t-1}) = 0.$$

8.1.2   Maximum Likelihood Estimation of GARCH Model with Jumps

The subsection describes quasi-maximum likelihood estimation (QML) of GARCH model with Jumps. The vector of model parameters is

$$\Theta = (\alpha_0, \alpha_1, \beta_1, \delta, \theta, a, b, c)^T.$$

We will assume that θ belongs to the set

$$S := \{(\alpha_0, \alpha_1, \beta_1, \delta, \theta, a, b, c)^T : \alpha_0 \geq 0, \ \alpha_1 > 0, \ \beta_1 > 0\}.$$

Denote

$$\Theta^* = (\alpha_0^*, \alpha_1^*, \beta_1^*, \delta^*, \theta^*, a^*, b^*, c^*)^T$$

the vector of the true values of parameters. The aim is to find Θ^* that maximize a QML function given an observation sequence

$$\epsilon_0, \ldots, \epsilon_n$$

of length n.

Define the sequence $(\tilde{\sigma}_1, \ldots, \tilde{\sigma}_n)$ by recursion:

$$\tilde{\sigma}_t^2 = \alpha_0 + \alpha_1 \epsilon_{t-1}^2 + \beta_1 \tilde{\sigma}_{t-1}^2.$$

If we assume that the likelihood function is Gaussian, then the log-likelihood function can be written as (see e.g. Chan and Maheu [2002]):

$$F_n(\Theta) := \sum_{t=1}^{n} \log f(\epsilon_t|I_{t-1}, \Theta),$$

where

$$f(\epsilon_t | I_{t-1}, \Theta) = \sum_{j=0}^{\infty} \frac{\exp(-\tilde{\lambda}_t)\tilde{\lambda}_t^j}{j!} f(\epsilon_t | n_t = j, I_{t-1}, \Theta) \qquad (8.4)$$

and

$$f(\epsilon_t | n_t = j, I_{t-1}, \Theta) = \frac{1}{\sqrt{2\pi(\tilde{\sigma}_t^2 + j\delta^2)}} \exp\left(-\frac{(\epsilon_t + \theta\lambda_t - \theta j)^2}{2(\tilde{\sigma}_t^2 + j\delta^2)}\right). \qquad (8.5)$$

The sequence of $\tilde{\lambda}_t$ is defined by recursion:

$$\tilde{\lambda}_t = a + b\tilde{\lambda}_{t-1} + c\zeta_{t-1},$$

where

$$\zeta_{t-1} = \mathbb{E}(n_{t-1} | I_{t-1}) - \tilde{\lambda}_{t-1},$$

and

$$\mathbb{E}(n_{t-1} | I_{t-1}) = \sum_{j=0}^{\infty} j P(n_{t-1} = j | I_{t-1}) =$$

$$= \sum_{j=0}^{\infty} j \frac{f(\epsilon_t | n_{t-1} = j, I_{t-2}, \Theta) P(n_{t-1} = j) | I_{t-2})}{f(\epsilon_t | I_{t-2}, \Theta)} =$$

$$= \frac{\sum_{j=1}^{\infty} \frac{\exp(-\tilde{\lambda}_{t-1})\tilde{\lambda}_{t-1}^j}{j!} \frac{1}{\sqrt{2\pi(\tilde{\sigma}_{t-1}^2 + j\delta^2)}} \exp\left(-\frac{(\epsilon_{t-1} + \theta\lambda_{t-1} - \theta j)^2}{2(\tilde{\sigma}_{t-1}^2 + j\delta^2)}\right)}{f(\epsilon_{t-1} | I_{t-2}, \Theta)} \qquad (8.6)$$

The maximum likelihood estimator of Θ is defined by

$$\Theta^* = \arg\max_{\Theta \in S} F_n(\Theta).$$

Since the densities (8.5) has an infinite sum, it is impossible to use them for parameters' estimation. There are two ways of using equation (8.5):

- taking a finite Taylor expansions of (8.5);
- truncation of the sum (8.5), i.e. limitation of the number of terms in the sum.

It is should be noted that the calibration problem is non convex and surface of optimized function has a highly complex relief. As it was mentioned in Chapter 3, finding its exact solution is a difficult task. We faced with difficulties when calibrate process via MATLAB function fminsearch. In particular, the calibration process is not robust and extremely sensitive to the choice of a starting point. For this reason, we do not include any empirical results for the GARCH model with jumps (the case of autoregressive jump intensity). However, if we would assume that jump intensity is constant over time then the calibration process converges.

8.1.3   Empirical Results

We use the data set described in Section 7.2. Dataset includes the daily stock closing prices of five companies traded on London Stock Exchange: AVIVA, BP, BT Group, Lloyd Banking Group, HSBC.

Table 7.1 shows preliminary descriptive statistics for the stock prices log returns.

Table 8.1 shows the maximum likelihood estimates of GARCH(1,1) model with Jumps (with constant jump intensity, i.e. it is assumed that $b = c = 0$) for log returns of the closing daily prices of the five companies for 3 years (July 5, 2005 - July 5, 2008).

Table 8.1: Maximum likelihood estimates of GARCH(1,1) model with Jumps for log returns of the closing daily prices

Company	α	β	δ	θ	λ	$\alpha + \beta$	LLF_6
AVIVA	0.1247	0.8248	1.44E-02	-9.66E-03	0.9496	0.9495	2804.88
BP	0.0918	0.7919	1.02E-02	4.95E-04	0.8837	0.8837	2875.06
BT Group	0.0406	0.9332	1.87E-02	1.05E-03	0.9738	0.9738	2825.57
Lloyds	0.1262	0.8464	1.45E-02	4.11E-04	0.9726	0.9726	2899.96
HSBC	0.1335	0.8278	1.56E-02	-6.52E-04	0.9613	0.9613	3126.34

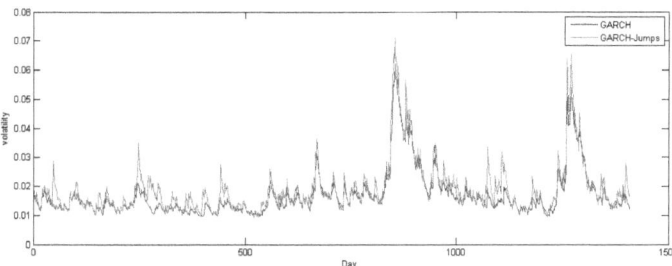

Figure 8.1: GARCH model and GARCH model with Jumps performance for BP stock market closing daily prices (January 5, 2005 - December 31, 2010)

8.2 Individual Stock Volatility Modelling With GARCH–Jumps Model Augmented With News Analytics Data

8.2.1 Model description

We are going to analyze the impact of news process intensity on stock volatility by extending GARCH-Jump models proposed and studied in Maheu and McCurdy [2004].

Let X_t be the log return of a particular stock or the market portfolio from time $t-1$ to time t. Let I_{t-1} denotes the past information set containing the realized values of all relevant variables up to time $t-1$. Suppose investors know the information in I_{t-1} when they make their investment decision at time $t-1$. Then the relevant expected return μ_t to the investors is the conditional expected value of X_t, given I_{t-1}, i.e.

$$\mu_t = E(X_t|I_{t-1}).$$

The relevant expected volatility σ_t^2 to the investors is conditional variance of X_t, given I_{t-1}, i.e.

$$\sigma_t^2 = Var(X_t|I_{t-1}).$$

Then

$$\epsilon_t = X_t - \mu_t$$

is the unexpected return at time t. Following Maheu and McCurdy [2004] we suppose that news process have two separate components: normal and unusual news,

$$\epsilon_t = \epsilon_{1,t} + \epsilon_{2,t}. \tag{8.7}$$

The first term in (8.7) reflects the impact of normal news to volatility:

$$\epsilon_{1,t} = \sigma_t u_t, t \in \mathbb{Z},$$

where (u_n) be a sequence of i.i.d. random variables such that $u_t \sim N(0,1)$, (σ_t) is a nonnegative process such that

$$\sigma_t^2 = \alpha_0 + \alpha_1 \epsilon_{t-1}^2 + \beta_1 \sigma_{t-1}^2$$

and

$$\alpha_0, \alpha_1, \beta_1 > 0.$$

The second term in (8.7) reflects the result of unexpected events and describe jumps in volatility:

$$\epsilon_{2,t} = \sum_{k=1}^{N_t} Y_{t,k} - \theta \lambda_t,$$

where $Y_{t,k} \sim \mathcal{N}(\theta, \delta^2)$, N_t is a Poisson random variable with conditional jump intensity

$$\lambda_t = a + b\lambda_{t-1} + c\zeta_{t-1} + \rho_1 n_{t-1}^+ + \rho_2 n_{t-1}^-,$$

where $\zeta_{t-1} = \mathbb{E}(N_{t-1}|I_{t-1}) - \theta \lambda_{t-1}$, and n_{t-1}^+, n_{t-1}^- is the number of positive and negative news from $t-2$ to $t-1$ respectively. Therefore we directly take into account the qualitative data of news intensity and news sentiment score (source: RavenPack News Scores).

8.2.2   Empirical results

Table 8.2 presents maximum likelihood estimates of GARCH(1,1)–Jumps model augmented with news intensity for log returns of the closing daily prices for the five companies (January 5, 2005 - December 31, 2010). It shows that $\rho_1 < \rho_2$ for all companies, i.e. the impact of the number of negative news on the growth of jump intensity much higher than one's of positive news.

Table 8.2: Maximum likelihood estimates of GARCH(1,1)–Jumps model augmented with news intensity for log returns of the closing daily prices

Company	α	β	δ	θ	λ	ρ_1	ρ_2	LLF_7
AVIVA	0.12	0.82	1.4E-02	-9.7E-03	0.14	0.011	0.12	2876.37
BP	0.09	0.79	1.0E-02	4.9E-04	0.58	0.032	0.42	3239.31
BT Group	0.04	0.93	1.9E-02	1.0E-03	0.26	0.03	0.42	2835.06
Lloyds	0.13	0.85	1.4E-02	4.1E-04	0.20	0.04	0.13	2909.35
HSBC	0.13	0.83	1.6E-02	-6.5E-04	0.06	0.00	0.01	3128.33

Note that the GARCH model with jumps (the null model) is a special case of the augmented GARCH-Jumps model (the alternative model). Therefore, to compare the fit of two models it can be used a likelihood ratio test (see e.g. Cox and Hinkley [1974]). Results of likelihood ratio test are in Table 8.3. For tree of five companies the alternative model is preferable with confidence level 5%.

Table 8.3: Results of the likelihood ratio test for the GARCH model with jumps and the augmented GARCH-Jumps model

Company	LLF_6	LLF_7	$2(LLF_7 - LLF_6)$	$\chi^2(2), 5\%$	Null Hyp.
AVIVA	2804.89	2876.37	142.96	5.99	rejected
BP	2875.06	3239.31	728.50	5.99	rejected
BT Group	2825.58	2835.06	18.96	5.99	rejected
Lloyds	2899.97	2909.35	18.77	5.99	rejected
HSBC	3126.34	3128.33	3.98	5.99	accepted

8.3 Summary

In the chapter we have examined two GARCH models with jumps. First we consider the well-known GARCH model with jumps proposed in Maheu and Mc-Curdy [2004]. Then we introduced the GARCH–Jumps model augmented with news intensity and obtained some empirical results. The main assumption of the model is that jump intensity might change over time and that jump intensity depends linearly on the number of positive and negative news. It is not clear whether news adds any value to a jump-GARCH model. However, the comparison of the values of log likelihood shows that the GARCH–Jumps model augmented with news intensity performs slightly better than "pure" GARCH or the GARCH model with Jumps.

Chapter 9

Stochastic Volatility Models

9.1 Stochastic Volatility Models

In recent years, there has been an increasing interest in the modelling of the dynamic evolution of the volatility for the financial time series in the framework of stochastic volatility (SV) models. In these models the volatility is modeled as an unobserved latent variable. SV models are attractive because:

1. they represent the behavior of financial prices rather well.

2. their statistical properties are easy to derive

3. Compared with the more popular GARCH models, they capture the main empirical properties of financial time series in a more appropriate way.

There are two main classes of models used to explain time-varying volatility: GARCH and SV. In both of them, volatility is a random process. The stochastic volatility (SV) model provides an alternative to the ARCH-type models of Engle (1982). In GARCH models, the link between the data and this volatility process is deterministic, whereas in SV models the volatility process incorporates an additional source of noise. Given a model, Bayes' rule can be used to infer the distribution of the volatility variable conditional on the data. In GARCH models, this distribution is singular (up to an initial condition). The deterministic link between the data and the volatility process posited by GARCH models is difficult to justify, either theoretically or empirically. However, it makes estimation and analysis of such models much simpler, justifying their widespread use. SV models are closely related to financial models often used to represent stock price. Stochastic volatility (SV) models may be used as a way to model the time-varying volatility of asset returns. Time series of asset returns feature some stylized facts, the most important being volatility clustering, which produces a slowly decreasing positive autocorrelation function of the squared returns. Another stylized fact is excess kurtosis of the distribution (with respect to the Gaussian distribution). In the context of Financial Econometrics they were first introduced by Taylor [1986].

9.1.1   Canonical SV model

First we consider the case of a constant volatility. We will assume that the derivative's underlying price follows a standard model for geometric a Brownian motion:

$$dS_t = \mu S_t dt + \sigma S_t dW_t,$$

where

- μ is the constant drift (i.e. expected return) of the security price,

- σ is the constant volatility,

- dW_t is a Wiener process.

In the stochastic volatility model we replace the constant volatility σ with a function V_t, that models the variance of S_t. This variance function can also be modeled as brownian motion. It should be noted that the form of V_t is determined by the particular SV model under consideration.

The SV models includes two random processes, the first one for observations, and the second one for latent volatilities. Stochastic volatility asset price dynamics results in the movements of the price of an asset S_t and its stochastic volatility V_t via a continuous time diffusion by a Brownian motion:

$$dS_t = \mu_S dt + \sigma_S exp(V_t/2)dW_{1t}, \tag{9.1}$$

$$V_t = \omega + \psi V_t dt + \sigma_V dW_{2t} \tag{9.2}$$

where

- S_t represents log price,
- V_t is the latent volatility process,
- W_{1t} and W_{2t} are (possibly correlated) Brownian motions.

Data arise in discrete time so it is natural to take Euler discretization of equation (9.1) and (9.2).

The simplest version of a SV model is given by

$$y_t = exp(h_{t-1}/2)\epsilon_t, \tag{9.3}$$

$$h_t = \omega + \phi h_{t-1} + \sigma_h \eta_t, \tag{9.4}$$

where

- y_t is a return measured as $y_t = ln(S_t/S_{t-1})$,
- h_t is the unobserved log-volatility of y_t,
- $\mu = \mu_S$,
- $\sigma_Y = \sigma_S$,
- $\phi = \psi + 1$,
- and ϵ_t and η_t are iid standard normal variables with $N(0,1)$ and are mutually independent,
- μ, ϕ, σ are parameters to be estimated, jointly denoted as θ.

The parameter ϕ is the persistence of the volatility process that also allows for the volatility clustering feature. The strict stationarity of y_t is ensured by the restriction on ϕ. Estimates of ϕ are usually quite close to 1.

The unconditional mean of log volatility h_t is equal to $\mu = \omega/(1 - \phi)$. Thus the second equation may be parameterized using μ. Then

$$y_t = exp(h_{t-1}/2)\epsilon_t,$$

$$h_t = \mu + \phi(h_{t-1} - \mu) + \sigma_h \eta_t$$

or

$$y_t = exp(h_{t-1}/2)\epsilon_t,$$

$$h_t = \mu(1 - \phi) + \phi h_{t-1} + \sigma_h \eta_t.$$

It is convenient to remove ω from second equation. In this case the model will take the form

$$y_t = \delta exp(h_{t-1}/2)\epsilon_t,$$

$$h_t = \phi h_{t-1} + \sigma_h \eta_t,$$

where $\delta = exp(\omega/2)$.

All of these parameterizations are equivalent. Which one to choose is mainly a matter of convenience.

9.1.2   Other univariate SV models

SV model with leverage effect

The financial leverage effect is an essential and well-known empirical fact observed in many financial time series. Many studies and research papers were devoted to the relationship between volatility and price/return. It is evident that bad news decrease the price and hence increase the debt-to-equity ratio (i.e. financial leverage). Therefore, bad news lead the firm to be riskier and push to increase future expected volatility. This phenomena describe the relationship between returns and conditional variances. It is plausible to think that bad news in the markets simultaneously leads price decrease and to an increase in the variance. On the other hand, periods of high volatility produce expectations of lower future returns, hence the negative correlation between these shocks. Leverage effect also plays an important part in the explanation of some of the characteristics of the data on the financial derivatives' markets.

Usually, the leverage effect manifests in a negative relationship between volatility and price/return. Nelson (1991) developed the framework for analysis of the leverage effect in the GARCH setting. Based on this empirical feature, Harvey et al. [1994] introduced a SV model with leverage effect. The model is referred as the asymmetric SV (ASV1) model. This model is the Euler approximation to the continuous time asymmetric SV model, which is well-known in the devoted to option price papers Hull and White [1987], Wiggins [1987], and Chesney and Scott [1989]. Harvey and Shephard (1996) treat the filtered volatility as a predictor of the return rate. Another approach also exists, in which the leverage effect is defined as a negative relationship between expected volatility and the return at period t. In the paper (Harvey and Shephard) the model is fitted to stock data using a quasi-maximum likelihood method. Jacquier et al. [2004] Jaquuier, Polson and Rossi (2004) provide an MCMC algorithm for the leverage stochastic volatility (SVL) model. Stochastic volatility framework has also been presented in Yu [2004]. Thus SV model is extended by including non-zero correlation ρ between ϵ_t and η_t from equations 9.3, 9.4. The model is specified as follows:

$$y_t = exp(h_{t-1}/2)\epsilon_t, \tag{9.5}$$

$$h_t = \omega + \phi h_{t-1} + \varphi \epsilon_t + \sigma_\eta \eta_t, \tag{9.6}$$

- $\varphi = \tau \rho$

- $\sigma_\eta^2 = \tau(1 - \rho^2)$

- ϵ_t, η_t are iid standard normal errors,

- $y_t = ln(S_t/S_{t-1})$ is the continuously compounded return,

- $\epsilon_t = W_1(t) - W_1(t - 1)$,

- $\eta_t = W_2(t) - W_2(t - 1)$.

Hence, ϵ_t and η_t are iid $N(0,1)$ and $cor(\epsilon_t, \eta_t) = \rho$. Compared with the basic SV model, a contemporaneous dependence is allowed in the ASV1 model. While $\rho < 0$ characterizes a leverage effect, negative shocks in observation y_t are associated with higher $h_{t+k}, k \geq 0$ and positive shock in y_t is associated with lower h_t. We assume that the initial state h_0, i.e. the volatility at time 0, is distributed according $N(\frac{\omega}{1-\phi}, \frac{\omega}{\sigma_\eta^2 - \phi^2})$, that is the invariant law of the autoregressive model, equal to the first two marginal moments of the underlying volatility process.

Fat-tailed distribution of error term

Since daily asset returns are leptokurtic, some researchers model stock returns as independent and identically distributed draws from fat-tailed distributions. On the other hand volatility changes over time. Therefore, the unconditional distribution of returns is leptokurtic even if the conditional distribution is normal. Changes on volatility cannot completely explain leptokurtosis of assets returns. The SV model with fat-tailed error can describe a wide range of kurtosis. This is important when we are dealing with outliers in the financial series. The SV model with fat-tailed error can be represented as

$$y_t = exp(h_{t-1}/2)\epsilon_t, \tag{9.7}$$

$$h_t = \omega + \phi h_{t-1} + \varphi U_t + \sigma_\eta \eta_t, \tag{9.8}$$

$$\epsilon_t = \sqrt{\lambda_t} z_t, \tag{9.9}$$

$$\lambda_t \sim IG(\nu/2, \nu/2) \tag{9.10}$$

so that $\epsilon_t \sim t_k(0,1)$ is a standard Student's t distribution with k degrees o freedom. Further particulars can be found in Griffin and Steel [2010], Omori et al. [2007], Asai [2008], Nakajima and Omori [2009], and Abanto-Valle et al. [2010] .

Long memory SV models.

Such models explain how persistent the volatility is, or how quickly financial markets forget large volatility shocks.

A observed property of many financial data series is that they appear to have
long memory, either in mean or in variance. This means that the results of shocks
on financial time series take a very long time to pass. The long memory property is well documented for various volatility measures (such as absolute returns, squared returns, an realized volatility for stock prices, foreign exchange
rates) (see. Taylor [1986] Taylor (1986), Ding, Granger, and Engle (1993), Dacorogna et al. [1993] , and Andersen et al. [2007] One way to model such behavior is through fractionally integrated time series processes. Long memory
in the conditional variance of financial data series is even more prevalent than
long memory in the mean. This has led to the development of fractionally integrated versions of both the GARCH and the stochastic volatility model. Models of conditional volatility lead to fractionally integrated GARCH and fractionally integrated stochastic volatility models. The stationary stochastic processes
such as LMSV are long-memory models for volatility. Jensen [2004] proposed a
long-memory SV model where the log-volatilities exhibit long memory properties (LMSV)

$$y_t = exp(h_{t-1}/2)\epsilon_t, \tag{9.11}$$
$$(1 - L)^d h_t = \sigma_\eta \eta_t, \tag{9.12}$$

where L is the lag operator.

SV model with jumps in returns

In the recent econometric literature, the basic SV model was extended in order to
take into account a jump's dynamic to describe extreme and rare events such as
crashes on the market. It is useful to introduce a jump component in the return
and in the volatility equations. Similar to the basic SV model, the Euler discretization of continuous time jump (SVJ) process leads to a specification of the form

$$y_t = exp(h_{t-1}/2)\epsilon_t + J_t z_t, \tag{9.13}$$
$$h_{t+1} = h_t + \phi h_{t-1} + \eta_t, \eta_t \sim N(0, \sigma_\eta^2), \tag{9.14}$$
$$J_t \sim Ber(\lambda), \tag{9.15}$$

$$z_t \sim N(\mu_z, \sigma_z^2), \tag{9.16}$$

where J_t is the indicator of a jump and Z_t the jump size. For the jump specification, one can conditionally conjugate prior structure for parameters $(\lambda, \mu_z, \sigma_z,^2)$, where $\lambda \sim Beta(a, b)$, $\mu_z \sim N(c, d)$ and $\sigma_z^2 \sim IG(\nu/2, \nu\sigma_z^2)$, respectively. Lopes and Polson [2010] discusses the choice $c = -3, d = 0.01$ and $a = 2, b = 100$. In that case the prior mean of standard deviation of λ is around 0.02. This prior specification predicts about five large negative jumps per year (250 trading days), whose magnitude is around -3 percent.

SV with jumps in volatility

Empirical evidence suggests that conditional volatility of returns demonstrates a number of visible jumps in a year. Duffie et al. [2000] provides evidence of positive jumps in volatility. The SV model with fat-tailed error can be represented as

$$y_t = exp(h_{t-1}/2)\epsilon_t, \tag{9.17}$$

$$h_{t+1} = h_t + \phi h_{t-1} + J_t z_t + \eta_t, \eta_t \sim N(0, \sigma_\eta^2), \tag{9.18}$$

$$J_t \sim Ber(\lambda), \tag{9.19}$$

$$z_t \sim N(\mu_z, \sigma_z^2), \tag{9.20}$$

where J_t is the indicator of jump and Z_t the jump size. For the jump specification, one can conditionally conjugate prior structure for parameters $(\lambda, \mu_z, \sigma_z,^2)$, where $\lambda \sim Beta(a, b)$, $\mu_z \sim N^+(0, d)$ (truncated normal distribution) and $\sigma_z^2 \sim IG(\nu/2, \nu\sigma_z^2)$, respectively.

Markov switch stochastic volatility

One of the most popular nonlinear time series models in the literature is the Markov switching or regime switching model (see Hamilton (1989)). This model can characterize the time series behaviors in different regimes or states by postulating multiple equations for each states. This model is able to capture more complex dynamic patterns by permitting switching between these states. An important aspect of the Markov switching model is that the switching mechanism is controlled by an unobservable state variable. The Markovian property postulates that the current value of the state variable depends on its immediate past value. It is assumed that state variables follow a first-order Markov chain.

In 1998, So So et al. [1998] introduces Markov switching to the stochastic volatility model. Time varying parameters could be incorporated in the SV model in the dynamics of the log volatility. Model becomes:

$$y_t = exp(h_t/2) + e_t, e_t \sim N(0, \sigma_e^2), \qquad (9.21)$$

$$h_{t+1} = \mu_{s,t} + \phi h_{t-1} + \eta_t, \eta_t \sim N(0, \sigma_\eta^2), \qquad (9.22)$$

$$p_{ij} = Pr(s_t = j | s_{t-1} = i), i, j = 1, ..., k \qquad (9.23)$$

$$\mu_{st} = \gamma_1 + \sum_{j=1}^{k} \gamma_j I_{ji}, \qquad (9.24)$$

and regime variables s_t follow a k-state first order Markov process. $I_{jt} = 1$ if $s_t \geq j$ and zero otherwise, $\gamma_i >= 0$ for $i > 1$.

9.1.3   Adding News to the SV Model

The canonical SV model is too restrictive, but makes it easy to include additional regressors. The mean of y_t is not necessarily equal to zero and may be a function of explanatory variables x_t:

$$y_t = exp(h_t/2)\epsilon_t + x_t^T \beta, \epsilon_t \sim N(0, 1), \qquad (9.25)$$

Exactly the same h_t may be a function of observable variables z_t in addition to its own lags:

$$h_{t+1} = \mu + \phi h_{t-1} + z_t^T \gamma + \eta_t, \qquad (9.26)$$

The impact of exogenous explanatory variables on volatility has been examined in the context of the GARCH model by several authors Baillie and Bollerslev [1989]; Lamoureax and Lastrapes [1990].

Such explanatory variables could be intervention dummies, seasonal components, or regressors like option implied volatility, trade volume data, etc.

The empirical validity of the SV model with explanatory variables has been examined elsewhere (Ghysels and Jasiak [1995], Hubalek and Posedel [2008]). Therefore, we considered models including the number of news as the first and the second equation.

SV Model with Exogenous Jump Process

$$Y_t = \epsilon_t \exp(h_t/2) + \delta_t J_t$$

$$h_{t+1} = \mu(1 - \phi) + \phi h_t + \sigma_h \eta_t$$

μ is drift in the state equation; σ^2 - variance of the error term; ϕ - persistence parameter; δ_t jump size; $J_t \in \{0, 1\}$ - an exogenous binary variable based on news flow; $\epsilon_t \sim \mathcal{N}(0, \sigma_Y^2)$, $\eta_t \sim \mathcal{N}(0, 1)$

SV Model with Exogenous Jumps in Return depends on Positive and Negative News Intensity

Let us assume that the size of the particular jump is proportional to the number of positive or negative news.

$$y_t = exp(h_t/2)\epsilon_t + \beta_1 N_t^+ + \beta_2 N_t^-, \epsilon_t \sim N(0, \sigma_e^2), \tag{9.27}$$

$$h_{t+1} = \mu + \phi h_{t-1} + \eta_t, \tag{9.28}$$

SV model with exogenous control process of news flow

$$Y_t = \epsilon_t \exp(h_t/2)$$

$$h_{t+1} = \mu(1 - \phi) + \phi h_t + \gamma \log N_t + \sigma_h \eta_t$$

μ - drift in the state equation; σ^2 - variance of the error term; ϕ - persistence parameter; N_t - index of news intensity; $\epsilon_t \sim \mathcal{N}(0, \sigma_Y^2)$, $\eta_t \sim \mathcal{N}(0, 1)$

Positive and Negative News Intensity in State Equation

Previous model could be elaborated by adding two separate variables for the number of positive and negative news:

$$y_t = exp(h_t/2)e_t, e_t \sim N(0, \sigma_e^2), \tag{9.29}$$

$$h_{t+1} = \mu + \phi h_{t-1} + \gamma_1 N_t^+ + \gamma_2 N_t^- + \eta_t, \tag{9.30}$$

9.2   Estimation

Stochastic volatility model belongs to a class of nonlinear non-Gaussian state space models. The returns y_t is an observed variable and logarithmic volatility h_t is a latent state of the system at time t. Likelihood function $L(\theta; \mathbf{y})$ for stochastic volatility models can not be expressed explicitly. The likelihood is a T-dimensional integration with respect to unknown latent volatilities and its analytical form is, in general, unknown. The parameter estimation of the SV model is not straight-forward due the intractable form of likelihood. Several estimation methods have been proposed, including the generalised method of moments, quasi-maximum likelihood, efficient method of moments and simulation likelihood. Estimation of the parameters of the canonical SV model may be done by the maximum likelihood (ML) method or by Bayesian inference. ML and, in principle, Bayesian estimation require to compute the likelihood function of an observed sample, which is a difficult task.

Canonical SV Model

The standard univariate SV model proposed by Taylor(1986) is

$$y_t = exp(h_{t-1}/2)\epsilon_t, \epsilon_t \sim NID(0, 1)$$

$$h_t = \omega + \phi h_{t-1} + \sigma_h \eta_t, \eta_t \sim N(0, 1)$$

$$h_0 \sim N(\frac{\omega}{1-\phi}, \frac{\sigma_\eta^2}{1-\phi^2}),$$

where y_t is the observation at time t, h_t - logarithmic volatility is assumed to follow a stationary AR(1) process. It is assumed that the parameter σ_η is positive and the persistent parameter $|\phi| < 1$ (is close to one for application). The observation errors $\epsilon_t \sim N(0, 1)$ captures the measurement and sampling errors, whereas the process error $\eta_t \sim N(0, 1)$ assesses the variation in the underlying volatility dynamics.

Let us assume $\mathbf{y} = (y_1, ..., y_T)$ to be the vector of observed log-returns, $\mathbf{h} = (h_1, ..., h_T)$ to be the vector of unobserved volatilities, $\Omega_t = (y_1, ..., y_t, h_1, ..., h_t)$, $\theta = (\sigma_\epsilon, \phi, \sigma_\eta)$ to be the set of parameters. The SV model can be regarded as a nonlinear state space model. So to evaluate the likelihood, we have to integrate out the latent log volatilities.

$$f(\mathbf{y}|\theta) = \int f(\mathbf{y}, \mathbf{h}|\theta)d\mathbf{h} = \int f(\mathbf{y}|\mathbf{h}, \theta)f(\mathbf{h}|\theta)d\mathbf{h} \qquad (9.31)$$

$$f(\mathbf{h}|\theta) = \frac{f(\mathbf{y}, \mathbf{h}|\theta)}{f(\mathbf{y}|\theta)} \qquad (9.32)$$

The log volatility h_t is specified by the AR(1) process with Gaussian innovation noise. The density functions of y_t given h_t and of h_t given h_{t-1} are

$$f(y_t|h_t) = \frac{1}{\sqrt{2\pi}}exp(-\frac{y_t^2}{2}exp(-h_t) - \frac{h_t^2}{2}), \qquad (9.33)$$

$$f(h_t|h_{t-1}) = \frac{1}{\sqrt{2\pi}}exp(-\frac{h_t - \omega - \phi h_{t-1}}{2\sigma_\eta^2}), \qquad (9.34)$$

respectively.

$$logf(y_t, h_t|\theta) = -\frac{1}{2}log(2\pi) - \frac{h_t}{2} - \frac{y_t^2}{2exp(h_t)} \qquad (9.35)$$

The multistep procedure for likelihood evaluation takes the following form. (i) one step ahead prediction of y_t

$$f(y_t|\mathbf{y}_{t-1}) = \int_{-\infty}^{\infty} f(y_t, h_t|\mathbf{y}_{t-1})dh_t =$$
$$= \int_{-\infty}^{\infty} f(y_t|h_t)f(h_t|\mathbf{y}_{t-1})dh_t \qquad (9.36)$$

(ii) updating of h_t

$$f(h_t|\mathbf{y}_t) = f(h_t|y_t, \mathbf{y}_{t-1}) =$$
$$= \frac{f(y_t, h_t|\mathbf{y}_{t-1})}{f(y_t|\mathbf{y}_{t-1})} = \qquad (9.37)$$
$$= \frac{f(y_t, h_t)f(h_t|\mathbf{y}_{t-1})}{f(y_t|\mathbf{y}_{t-1})}$$

(iii) one step ahead prediction of h_t:

$$f(h_{t+1}|\mathbf{y}_t) = \int_{-\infty}^{\infty} f(h_{t+1}, h_t|\mathbf{y}_t)dh_t =$$
$$= \int_{-\infty}^{\infty} f(h_{t+1}|h_t)f(h_t|\mathbf{y}_t)dh_t \qquad (9.38)$$

If we have $f(y_t|\mathbf{y}_{t-1}), t = 1, ..., T$, we can calculate the log likelihood

$$L(\theta|\mathbf{y}_t) = \sum_{t=1}^{T} log f(y_t|\mathbf{y}_{t-1}) \qquad (9.39)$$

The logarithms of the densities of the components are given

$$log f(y_t|h_t, \theta) = -\frac{1}{2}log(2\pi) - \frac{h_t}{2} - \frac{y_t^2}{2\sigma_\eta^2 exp(h_t)} \qquad (9.40)$$

$$logf(h_t|h_t - 1, \theta) = -\frac{1}{2}log(2\pi\sigma_\eta^2) + \frac{\omega}{2\sigma_\eta^2} - \frac{1}{2\sigma_\eta^2}(h_t - h_{t-1})^2 \qquad (9.41)$$

$$logf(h_1|\theta) = -\frac{1}{2}log(2\pi\sigma_\eta^2) + \frac{1}{2}log(1 - \phi^2) - (\frac{h_1 - \frac{\omega}{1-\phi}}{\frac{\sigma_\eta^2}{1-\phi^2}})^2 \qquad (9.42)$$

It is difficult to solve the integrations in equations (9.37) and (9.39) analytically, because the SV model is not a linear Gaussian state space model.

An analytical solution to the integration problem is not available. Simulation methods are therefore used. Two methods directly approximate (9.39): efficient importance sampling (EIS), and Monte Carlo maximum likelihood (MCML). In this study we will use QML estimation, while other methods (MCML and EIS) are to be used in later investigations to enable us to compare results.

9.2.1   Linear Filtering and QML Estimation

Despite a very simple representation, standard SV model captures most of the empirical regularities found in financial time series.

An attractive feature of specification is the possibility of linearizing the model. By taking logarithms of the squared mean adjusted returns one obtains:

$$log(y_t^2) = \mu + h_t + \xi_t, \qquad (9.43)$$

$$h_t^2 = \omega + \phi h_{t-1} + \epsilon_t, \qquad (9.44)$$

where $\mu = log(y_t^2) + E(log(\epsilon_t^2))$, $h_t = log(\sigma_t^2)$, $\xi_t = log(\epsilon_t^2) - E(log(\epsilon_t^2))$. Model (9.43), (9.44), is non-Gaussian linear state space model. The property of measurement error ξ_t depend on the distribution of ϵ_t. If the original mean equation disturbance, ϵ_t, is standard normal, ξ_t follows the $log\chi_1^2$ distribution whose mean and variance are known to be -1.27 and $\pi^2/2$, respectively Broto and Ruiz [2004]. However the approximating model replaces this with a Gaussian distribution (defined below), keeping the state equation unchanged. Therefore, the whole machinery of the Kalman filter is applicable to the approximating model, which is a Gaussian linear state space model.

Harvey et al. (1994) suggested a Quasi-Maximum Likelihood (QML) method of estimating the model based on the Kalman filter.

Assuming joint conditional normality of (ξ_t, η_t) in equations (9.43), (9.44) represents the measurement and transition equations of the general linear state space model.

Once the model is in the state space form, the advantages of this approach become evident:

(i) explanatory variables can be easily incorporated into the variance equation,

(ii) more general ARMA processes can be assumed for the evolution of the latent variable,

(iii) missing or irregularly spaced observations can be handled,

(iv) it is be possible to examine the impact of exogenous explanatory variables and

(v) generalisations to the multivariate case are straightforward.

The disadvantages

- ξ_t is far from being Gaussian;
- the QML estimator is likely to have poor small sample properties even though it is consistent.

When returns y_t are very close to zero, the log-squared transformation yields large negative numbers. To solve this problem the following modification of log-squared transformation may be used

$$y_t^* = log(y_t^2 + \tau s^2) - \frac{\tau s^2}{y_t^2 + \tau s^2},\tag{9.45}$$

where s^2 is the sample variance of y_t and τ is a small constant Bollerslev and Wright. [2001]. To increase conversion speed of the estimation procedure, we subtracted the mean value from the our variable $\tilde{y}_t^* = y_t^* - \overline{y}^*$, because in this case significantly fewer iterations are needed to find a solution, and estimates practically coincide with the case when centering was not carried out.

Even though this method is not perfect, the QML procedure is very flexible and has been successfully implemented for empirical analysis of stock price returns and other financial data. In addition, is is easy to add more explanatory variables to the model and then apply QML.

Chapter 10

Empirical Results

10.1 Empirical Results for Canonical SV Model

We examine the following stochastic volatility model with uncorrelated measurement errors and state equation with exogenous control process of news flow ((9.43), (9.44), (9.45)):

$$y_t^* = \mu + h_t + \delta_t,$$
$$h_{t+1} = \omega + \phi h_t + \sigma_h \eta_t$$
$$y_t^* = log(y_t^2 + \tau s^2) - \frac{\tau s^2}{y_t^2 + \tau s^2},$$

where s^2 is the sample variance of y_t and $\tau = 0.02$. Also, we apply a preliminary transformation as described in the previous section (3.2).

The data series consists of 1450 daily contionously compounded return, $lr_{it} = logp_t - logp_{t-1}$ from July 6, 2005 to December 31, 2010 for 92 company from FTSE100.

As an example, we briefly discuss the results for GB/ABF (Associated British Foods PLC). The time series plot is presented on Figure 10.1. The annualized

Table 10.1: Parameter estimates for basic SV model for GB/ABF

y	Coef.	Std. Err.	z	$Prob > \|z\|$	$95\% Conf.$	Interval
h						
h_{t-1}	.9692545	.0118645	81.69	0.000	.9460005	.9925086
cons	-.0012459	.0100107	-0.12	0.901	-.0208665	.0183746
σ_η^2	.1381055	.0560022	2.47	0.014	.0283433	.2478677
σ_ξ^2	3.208062	.1290949	24.85	0.000	2.955041	3.461083

mean and annualized standard deviation of the data are 0.018% and 1.406%, respectively. The data exhibits the negative skewness with value -0.165, and kurtosis is 7.555. Skewness/Kurtosis test rejects hypothesis of normality.

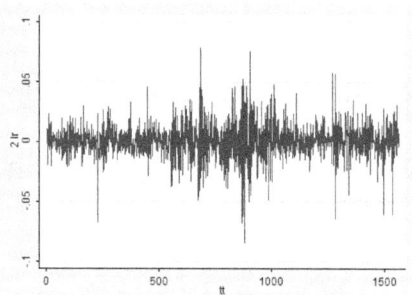

Figure 10.1: Log return for GB/ABF

The Box-Luing's serial correlation test on the absolute returns shows that absolute returns are not independently distributed, but decay geometrically with lag (Figure 10.2).

The results of the quasi-maximum likelihood parameter estimate can be found in Table 10.1.

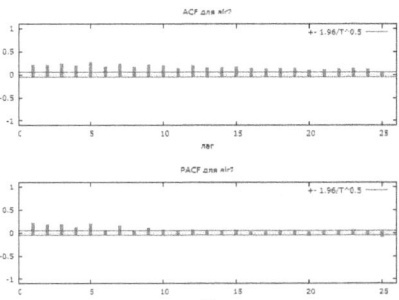

Figure 10.2: The sample ACF for daily absolute returns for GB/ABF stock price for the period July 2006 - December 2010

Estimate of ϕ is equal to 0.969. It indicates that the volatility process is highly persistent. This evidence is consistent with stylized facts on stock return. Figure 10.4 shows the predicted implied volatility. Figures 10.1 show that the estimated volatility has similar movement as $|y_t|$.

Similar results were obtained for most of the analyzed time series of stock returns. Only for a few companies low values of persistence were obtained. For example, for $GB/AU.$ company the estimated value of parameter ϕ is equal to 0.6739. The estimates of SV model for some companies are presented in Table 10.2.

Perhaps this is due to the fact that the upward trend for stock prices was typical for that company.

10.2   Empirical Results for SV model with exogenous control process of news

Consider the extended SV model:

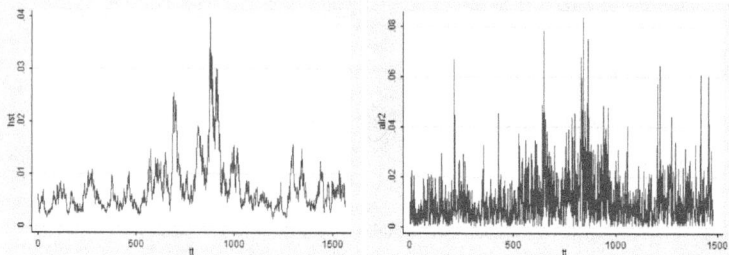

Figure 10.3: SV model. The esimated volatility and abs(return) for GB/ABF

Table 10.2: Estimation Results of Parameters of Canonical SV Model

Company	ϕ	ω	σ_η^2	σ_ξ^2
GB/BARC	0.987	-0.002	0.148	2.522
GB/BATS	0.982	-0.001	0.061	3.258
GB/LLOY	0.996	-0.002	0.051	2.602
GB/MKS	0.992	-0.002	0.043	3.141
GB/RDSA	0.989	-0.001	0.040	3.115
GB/RR.	0.985	0.000	0.071	3.316

$$y_t = exp(h_{t-1}/2)\epsilon_t, \tag{10.1}$$

$$h_t = \omega + \phi h_{t-1} + \alpha_1 D_t^+ + \alpha_2 D_t^- + \sigma_\eta \eta_t, \tag{10.2}$$

where variables D_t^+, D_t^- denote the dummy variables for days with abnormal numbers of positive and negative news items at day t respectively.

Some companies has have much greater news coverage than the others. Therefore, the rule of labelling the days with abnormal news intensity depends on the company. For companies with small news intensity it can be days with only one piece of news. For companies with high news intensity (e.g. HSBC, BT, BP) we labeled day if the number of news in this day was two times higher then average news intensity level.

For GB/ABF company the news intensity is small. So we use a simple rule: a day is labelled if at least one piece of positive (negative) news came. The number of days, when at least one piece of positive news was recorded for GB/ABF, is equal to 223. The number of days with at least one negative news item is equal to 95.

The results of the quasi-maximum likelihood parameter estimation can be found in Table 10.3.

Table 10.3: Parameter estimates for extended SV model with dummy variable in state equation for GB/ABF

	Coef.	Std. Err.	z	$Prob > |z|$	$95\%Conf.$	Interval
h						
h_{t-1}	0.966	0.012	78.14	0.000	0.941	0.990
D^+	0.113	0.110	1.03	0.305	-0.103	0.329
D^-	0.328	0.163	2.00	0.045	0.006	0.649
cons	-0.041	0.02	-1.88	0.060	-0.084	0.001
σ_η^2	0.116	0.046	2.48	0.013	0.0243	0.207
σ_ξ^2	2.764	0.113	24.34	0.000	2.541	2.987

It is interesting to compare the results obtained if dummy variables are included in the observed equation (see Table 10.4 and Table 10.5).

Direct inclusion of the news in the state equation does not significantly improve the quality of the model. The hypothesis that their coefficients are zero is rejected for more then half of the FTSE100 companies. However, if we include the news in the observation equation, then the hypothesis of equality of the coefficients to zero is rejected for most of FTSE100 companies.

Instead of dummy variables we also can include the number of arriving news in the SV model :

$$y_t = exp(h_{t-1}/2)\epsilon_t, \tag{10.3}$$

$$h_t = \omega + \phi h_{t-1} + \beta_1 N_t^+ + \beta_2 N_t^- + \sigma_\eta \eta_t, \tag{10.4}$$

where variables N_t^+, N_t^- denote the logarithm of numbers of positive and negative news items at day t respectively.

Table 10.4: Parameter estimates for extended SV model with dummy variable in observation equation for GB/ABF

	Coef.	Std. Err.	z	$Prob > |z|$	$95\%Conf.$	Interval
h						
h_{t-1}	0.976	0.010	98.81	0.000	0.957	0.996
cons	-0.005	0.008	-0.59	0.557	-0.022	0.012
y						
D^+	0.379	0.108	3.52	0.000	0.168	0.590
D^-	0.255	0.202	1.26	0.207	-0.141	0.651
σ_η^2	0.092	0.038	2.42	0.016	0.017	0.167
σ_ξ^2	2.742	0.112	24.51	0.000	2.523	2.961

Table 10.5: Estimation Results of Parameters of SV Model with News in Observations Equation

$Company$	ϕ	β_1	β_2	ω	σ_η^2	σ_ξ^2
GB/BARC	0.988	-0.004	0.164	0.511	0.125	2.506
GB/BATS	0.987	-0.003	0.352	0.601	0.042	3.242
GB/LLOY	0.996	-0.003	0.445	0.459	0.041	2.570
GB/MKS	0.994	-0.004	0.496	0.855	0.031	3.040
GB/RDSA	0.989	-0.002	0.190	0.222	0.040	3.103
GB/RR.	0.987	-0.003	0.388	0.490	0.059	3.292

In Table 10.6 and Table 10.7 we report the estimates of parameters for the model (10.3), (10.4).

Estimates of predicted volatility for basic and extended models are close enough (Figure 10.5). Note that the direct incorporation of the news in the equation of state does not significantly improve the accuracy of the model.

In our opinion, the small impact of news intensity on stock volatility might be connected with the fact that we considered only the company-specific news. It

Table 10.6: Parameter estimates for extended SV model with logarithm of number positive (negative) news items in state equation for GB/ABF

	Coef.	Std. Err.	z	$Prob > |z|$	95%$Conf.$	Interval
h						
h_{t-1}	0.965	0.012	81.34	0.000	0.942	0.988
N^+	0.139	0.096	1.44	0.149	-0.050	0.327
N^-	0.337	0.172	1.96	0.050	0.000	0.675
cons	-0.046	0.019	-2.46	0.014	-0.083	-0.009
σ_η^2	0.111	0.044	2.53	0.012	0.025	0.197
σ_ξ^2	2.766	0.113	24.42	0.000	2.544	2.988

Table 10.7: Estimation Results of Parameters of SV Model with Lagged News in State Equation

Company	ϕ	β_1	β_2	ω	σ_η^2	σ_ξ^2
GB/BARC	0.9678	-0.0607	0.2453	-0.0603	0.1796	2.5021
GB/BATS	0.9508	0.1065	0.268	-0.0535	0.17	3.1601
GB/LLOY	0.9911	0.0424	0.0215	-0.0244	0.0732	2.5721
GB/MKS	0.9648	0.0575	0.3415	-0.0636	0.1403	3.0253
GB/RDSA	0.9906	0.0458	-0.0335	-0.0211	0.0284	3.1324
GB/RR.	0.9795	-0.0598	0.1609	0.0205	0.0797	3.3095

is possible that their impact is short-term. Notice that specifications of models (10.1), (10.1) or (10.3), (10.4) imply that the impact of news intensity on stock volatility is long-term, i.e. the impact holds not only for the current day but also for several days after that. We consider the possible modification of stochastic volatility model with an exogenous flow of news.

Assume that at the time moment t we have $N_t^+ \neq 0, N_t^- = 0, N_{t+1}^+, N_{t+1}^- = 0$. It follows from (10.4) that the value of the state variable at the time moment $t+1$ is equal to

$$
\begin{aligned}
h_{t+1} =& \omega + \phi h_t + \sigma_\eta \eta_{t+1} = \\
& \omega + \phi(\omega + \phi h_t + \beta_1 N_t^+ + \sigma_\eta \eta_t) + \sigma_\eta \eta_t = \\
& (1 + \phi)\omega + \phi\beta_1 N_t^+ + \phi\sigma_\eta \eta_t + \sigma_\eta \eta_{t+1} =
\end{aligned}
\tag{10.5}
$$

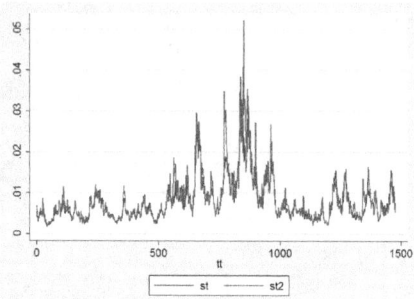

Figure 10.4: The estimated volatility for SV model and SV model with news in state equation for GB/ABF

Thus, the impact of news shock on stock volatility decays exponentially. It may be possible to derive the time of the decay of shocks, τ, from the inequality:

$$\beta_1 \phi^\tau < c,$$

where level c is a given as a real positive number.

In chapter 2.3 we found that news is more likely to lead to short-term jump in returns than to long-term change of volatility. We can suggest the following way of testing this hypothesis. Let us include additional variables N_{t-1}^+, N_{t-1}^- to the model.

$$y_t = exp(h_{t-1}/2)\epsilon_t, \tag{10.6}$$

$$h_t = \omega + \phi h_{t-1} + \beta_1 N_t^+ + \beta_2 N_t^- + \gamma_1 N_{t-1}^+ + \gamma_2 N_{t-1}^- + \sigma_\eta \eta_t, \tag{10.7}$$

If the impact of news is short-term, then the jump of volatility in the previous day would be amortized in the current day. Thus, the parameter γ_1 should be equal to $-\phi * \beta_1$. The hypothesis of short-term impact of positive and negative news on stock volatility can be written as

Table 10.8: Estimation Results of Parameters of SV Model with News in State Equation

Company	ϕ	β_1	β_2	γ_1	γ_2	ω	σ_η^2	σ_ξ^2	χ_W^2
GB/ABF	0.965	0.254	0.418	-0.271	-0.112	-0.017	0.129	3.216	3.00
GB/BARC	0.985	0.099	0.222	-0.189	-0.114	0.037	0.119	2.538	1.61
GB/BATS	0.980	0.156	0.303	-0.103	-0.312	-0.017	0.062	3.251	2.15
GB/LLOY	0.998	0.269	0.223	-0.258	-0.250	0.001	0.038	2.609	1.33
GB/MKS	0.992	0.157	0.496	-0.184	-0.456	0.003	0.040	3.125	1.06
GB/RDSA	0.990	0.261	0.213	-0.229	-0.254	-0.007	0.032	3.105	3.90
GB/RR.	0.982	-0.006	0.639	-0.080	-0.573	0.040	0.068	3.308	2.80

$$H_0 : \begin{cases} \beta_1 = -\phi\gamma_1, \\ \beta_2 = -\phi\gamma_2. \end{cases} \tag{10.8}$$

Empirical results can be found in Table 10.8. It is interesting that estimates of parameters β_1, β_2 (the current day) are positive, while estimates of parameters γ_1, γ_2 (the prevoious day) are negative. Moreover they are significant.

It is worth noting that hypothesis 10.8 is not rejected for almost all FTSE100 companies. We use the Wald test for linear restriction on coefficients (see column χ^2 in Table C.4 of Appendix). As example, the results indicate that we cannot reject the null hypothesis for GB/ABF company:

$$H_0 : \begin{cases} \beta_1 + \gamma_1 = 0 \\ \beta_2 + \gamma_2 = 0, \end{cases} \quad \chi_{obs}^2 = 3.00 < \chi^2(0.05, 2) = 5.99 \tag{10.9}$$

Persistence of the extended SV model is slightly less than persistence of the basic SV model. For most of the companies estimates of the regression coefficients for negative news are statistically significant, while the same estimates of positive news are mainly insignificant. To be precise, coefficients for positive news are insignificant for companies. More than that, absolute value of the negative news coefficients is generally greater than that for positive news coefficients. We interpret this as an empirical rule: in general, negative news have more impact on

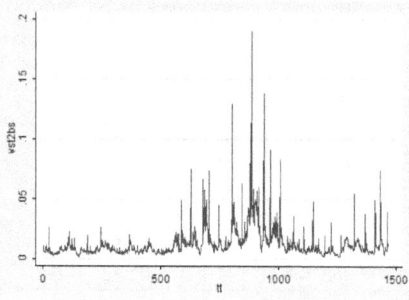

Figure 10.5: The estimated volatility for SV model with news in state equation for GB/ABF

jump sizes. Figure 10.5 shows the estimated volatility based on SV model with news intensity. The estimated volatility has some number of jumps.

Figure 10.6 presents days and size of jumps. Average jump size of the days t seems be proportional to current volatilities at the day t.

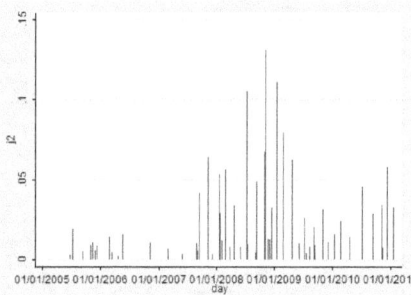

Figure 10.6: SV model with news in state equation for GB/ABF. Estimated jump size.

Chapter 11

Summary and future work

11.1 Summary and contributions

The first part of the thesis compares the performance of different GARCH models using backtesting procedures based on unconditional coverage test (Kupiec's test) and the test of conditional coverage.

The data set we have analyzed in this part of the work is the stock market closing daily prices of General Electric Company (GEC.L). The sample period is from January 2, 2008 to December 31, 2010. Data set are taken from UK Stock Market FTSE100 and downloaded from Yahoo!Finance site. The sample is divided in twelve parts for two purposes: in-sample estimation procedure and out-of-sample evaluation. Using the Jarque–Bera test statistics with 1% level we reject the null hypothesis of normality of log return series. Shapiro–Wilk W test also rejects the hypothesis of normal distribution of the data.

It was shown that the ARCH(1), GARCH (1, 1), TGARCH(1,1) and GJR-GARCH (1, 1) models calibrated on data sets of 1-year length (January 2, 2009 - December 31, 2009) under the normal distribution performed well. However, for 95% and 99% VaR estimations all the ARCH(1), GARCH (1, 1), TGARCH(1,1) and GJR-GARCH (1, 1) models calibrated on datasets of 2-year length (January 2, 2008 -

December 31, 2009) underestimated the risk and was rejected. It might be explained by huge difference in the level of volatility in 2008 crisis year compare with the one in 2009 year.

The second part of the work tries to evaluate the impact of news on stock volatility. There are not so much research works studying quantitative impact of news on stock volatility. It is worth to be mentioned the pioneering works Kalev et al. [2004] and Janssen [2004]. In the second of the papers the author examines impact of news releases on *index* volatility, while in our work we analyze the impact on *stock* volatility following study of Kalev et al. [2004]. However, we restrict our choice by some of the FTSE100 companies, while Kalev et al. [2004] considered some French companies.

In the Chapter 5.5 we have tried to study different GARCH models augmented with news analytics data. The main goal was to examine the impact of news intensity on stock volatility. Based on empirical evidences for some of FTSE100 companies it has been shown that the GARCH(1,1) model augmented with volume does remove GARCH and ARCH effects for most of the FTSE100 companies, while the GARCH(1,1) model augmented with news intensity has difficulties in removing the effects. It has been shown that the GARCH(1,1) model augmented with the news intensity n_t (the number of daily announcements) does not necessarily remove GARCH and ARCH effects. However, the likelihood ratio test has shown that the GARCH(1,1) model augmented with the news intensity performs better than the "pure" GARCH model.

Then we compare GARCH model with jumps and GARCH–Jumps model augmented with news intensity using likelihood ratio test.

To calibrate the models we have used the Maximum Likelihood Estimation (MLE) and Quasi Maximum Likelihood Estimation (QMLE) methods. The volatility models are calibrated on the software package MATLAB. We used RavenPack news analytics data.

11.2 Future work

The study has shown that the problem of examining the impact of news intensity on stock volatility is far more sophisticated than it might seem at first sight. The empirical results show that there are no strong arguments in support of hypothesis of impact of news intensity on volatility. It might be occur due the following causes:

- an additional preprocessing of news analytics data is required;

- the models do not take into account macro economics news;

- it could be seen the splash of volatility in 2008, while news intensity has not been changing very much over the whole period;

- news intensity might not affect volatility directly, although jumps in returns could be caused by news releases.

The work may be considered as a preliminary work on the problem of evaluation of impact of news on stock volatility. Based on the research it can be suggested some directions of future work.

- The first problem is to develop a GARCH-type model with news analytics data for prediction VaR with better performance than the "pure" GARCH model.

- It is worth considering the problem of mutual dependence of volatility and news intensity.

- The problem of calibration of augmented models (e.g. GARCH–Jumps models) is difficult due to its non convexity and noisiness (the problem was mentioned in Chapter 8). We can try to use different solvers for global optimization or to develop new algorithms.

Future work may be also associated with the study of

- *Markov – Switching GARCH models.* The idea is to estimate a model that permits regime switching in the parameters caused by movements of news intensity. It is a generalization of the GARCH model and permits a different persistence in the conditional variance of each regime. Thus, the conditional variance in each regime accommodates volatility clustering, nesting the GARCH model as special case.

- *HMM – GARCH Model.* The model is similar to the previous one, but it is supposed that the process is a hidden Markov process. We will suppose that the hidden states in HMM are "somehow" connected with observable sequence of the news sentiment score and parameters of GARCH model are state-dependant.

There are some evidences (see e.g. Mitra and Mitra [2011]) that effect of news on prices is short-term, therefore it is more likely that we need tick by tick data to examine impact of news on stock volatility.

List of Figures

List of Tables

Bibliography

C.A. Abanto-Valle, D. Bandyopadhyay, V.H. Lachos, and I. Enriquez. Robust bayesian analysis of heavy-tailed stochastic volatility models using scale mixtures of normal distributions. *Computational Statistics & Data Analysis*, 54(12): 2883–2898, December 2010.

T. G. Andersen. Return volatility and trading volume: An information flow interpretation of stochastic volatility. *Journal of Finance*, 51:169–204, 1996.

T.G. Andersen, T. Bollerslev, and F.X. Diebold. Roughing it up: Including jump components in the measurement, modeling, and forecasting of return volatility. *The Review of Economics and Statistics*, 89(4):701–720, 04 2007.

V. Arago and L. Nieto. Heteroskedasticity in the returns of the mainword stock exchange indices: volume versus garch effects. *International Financial Markets Institute and Money*, 15:271–284, 2005.

M. Asai. Autoregressive stochastic volatility models with heavy-tailed distributions: A comparison with multifactor volatility models. *Journal of Empirical Finance*, 15(2):332–341, March 2008.

R. T. Baillie and T. Bollerslev. Common stochastic trends in a system of exchange rates. *Journal of Finance*, 44(1):167–81, March 1989.

R. Bauer and F. Nieuwland. A multiplicative model for volume and volatility. *Applied Mathematical Finance*, 2:135–154, 1995.

T. D. Berry and K. M. Howe. Public information arrival. *Journal of Finance*, 49: 1331–1346, 1993.

F. Black. Studies in stock price volatility changes. In *Proceedings of the Business and Economic Statistics Section*, pages 177–181. American Statistical Association, 1976.

T. Bollerslev. Generalized autoregressive conditional heteroskedasticity. *Journal of Econometrics*, 31:307–327, 1986.

T. Bollerslev. Arch modeling in finance: A review of the theory and empirical evidence. *Journal of Econometrics*, 52:5–59, 1992.

T. Bollerslev and J. H. Wright. High-frequency data, frequency domain inference, and volatility forecasting. *The Review of Economics and Statistics*, 83(4):596–602, November 2001.

T. A Bollerslev. Conditionally heteroskedastic time series model for security prices and rates of return data. *Review of Economics and Statistics*, 69:542–547, 1987.

C. Broto and E. Ruiz. Estimation methods for stochastic volatility models: a survey. *Journal of Economic Surveys*, 18(5):613–649, December 2004.

W. H. Chan and J. M. Maheu. Conditional jump dynamics in stock market returns. *Journal of Business and Economic Statistics*, 20(3):377–389, 2002.

M. Chesney and L. Scott. Pricing european currency options: A comparison of the modified black-scholes model and a random variance model. *Journal of Financial and Quantitative Analysis*, 24(03):267–284, September 1989.

P. Christoffersen. Evaluating interval forecasts. *International Economic Review*, 39: 841–862, 1998.

P. K. Clark. A subordinated stochastich process model with finite variance for speculative prices. *Econometrica*, 41:135–155, 1973.

J.-G. Cousin and T. de Launois. News intensity and conditional volatility on the french stock market. *Finance*, 27:7–60, 2006.

D. R. Cox and D. V Hinkley. *Theoretical Statistics*. Chapman and Hall, 1974.

M.M. Dacorogna, U.A. Muller, R.J. Nagler, R. B. Olsen, and O.V. Pictet. A geographical model for the daily and weekly seasonal volatility in the foreign exchange market. *Journal of International Money and Finance*, 12(4):413–438, August 1993.

D. Duffie, J. Pan, and K. Singleton. Transform analysis and asset pricing for affine jump-diffusions. *Econometrica*, 68(6):1343–1376, November 2000.

L. H. Ederington and J. H. Lee. How markets process information: News releases and volatility. *Journal of Finance*, 48:1161–1191, 1993.

R. F. Engle. Autoregressive conditional heteroscedasticity with estimates of variance of united kingdom inflation. *Econometrica*, 50:987–1008, 1982.

R. F. Engle and V. K. Ng. Measuring and testing the impact of news on volatility. *Journal of Finance*, 48:174961777, 1993.

T. Epps and M. Epps. The stochastic dependence of stochastic price changes and transaction volume: Implications for the mixture of distribution hypothesis. *Econometrica*, 44:305–321, 1976.

K. R. French, G. W. Schwert, and R. F. Stambaugh. Expected stock returns and volatility. *Journal of Financial Economics*, 19:3–29, 1987.

E. Ghysels and J. Jasiak. Stochastic volatility and time deformation: An application to trading volume and leverage effects. CIRANO Working Papers 95s-31, CIRANO, June 1995.

L. R. Glosten, R. Jagannathan, and D. E. Runkle. On the relation between the expected value and the volatility of the nominal excess return on stocks. *Journal of Finance*, 48:1779–1801, 1993.

J.E. Griffin and M.F.J. Steel. Bayesian inference with stochastic volatility models using continuous superpositions of non-gaussian ornstein-uhlenbeck processes. *Computational Statistics & Data Analysis*, 54(11):2594–2608, November 2010.

A. R. Hall. *Generalized Method of Moments*. Oxford University Press, 2004.

P. Hansen and A. Lunde. A forecast comparison of volatility models: Does anything beat a garch (1,1)? working paper, Department of Economics, Brown University, 2001.

L. Harris. Transaction data tests of the mixture of distributions hypothesis. *Journal of Financial and Quantitative Analysis*, 22:127–141, 1987.

A. Harvey, E. Ruiz, and N. Shephard. Multivariate stochastic variance models. *Review of Economic Studies*, 61(2):247–64, April 1994.

F. Hubalek and P. Posedel. Joint analysis and estimation of stock prices and trading volume in barndorff-nielsen and shephard stochastic volatility models. Quantitative Finance Papers 0807.3464, arXiv.org, July 2008.

J. C. Hull and A. D. White. The pricing of options on assets with stochastic volatilities. *Journal of Finance*, 42(2):281–300, June 1987.

E. Jacquier, N.G. Polson, and P.E. Rossi. Bayesian analysis of stochastic volatility models with fat-tails and correlated errors. *Journal of Econometrics*, 122:185–212, April 2004.

G. Janssen. Public information arrival and volatility persistence in financial markets. *The European Journal of Finance*, 10:177–197, 2004.

M.J. Jensen. Semiparametric bayesian inference of long-memory stochastic volatility models. *Journal of Time Series Analysis*, 25(6):895–922, November 2004.

Ph. Jorion. *Value at Risk: The New Benchmark for Managing Financial Risk*. McGraw-Hill, 2 edition, 2001.

P. S. Kalev, W.-M. Liu, P. K. Pham, and E. Jarnecic. Public information arrival and volatility of intraday stock returns. *Journal of banking and Finance*, 28(6): 1447–1467, 2004.

M. Kantardzic. *Data Mining: Concepts, Models, Methods, and Algorithms*. John Wiley & Sons, 2003.

J. M. Karpoff. The relation between price changes and trading volume: A survey. *Journal of Financial and Quantitative Analysis*, 22:109–126, 1987.

S. Klarman. Beta. *ISI Review*, 5(117):309–327, 1991.

P. Kupiec. Techniques for verifying the accuracy of risk management models. *Journal of Derivatives*, 3:73–84, 1995.

C. G. Lamoureax and W. D. Lastrapes. Heteroskedasticity in stock return data: volume versus garch effects. *Journal of Business & Economic Statistics*, 2:253–260, 1990.

C. G. Lamoureax and W. D. Lastrapes. Endogenous trading volume and momentum in stock-return volatility. *Journal of Finance*, 45:221–229, 1991.

L. Le Cam. Maximum likelihood - an introduction. *ISI Review*, 58(2):153–171, 1990.

H.F. Lopes and N.G. Polson. *Rethinking Risk Measurement and Reporting: Uncertainty, Bayesian Analysis and Expert Judgement*, chapter Bayesian inference for stochastic volatility modeling, pages 515–551. Risk Books, 2010.

J. M. Maheu and T. H. McCurdy. News arrival, jump dynamics, and volatility components for individual stock returns. *Journal of Finance*, 59(2):755–793, 2004.

M. L. Mitchell and J. H. Mulherin. How markets process information: News releases and volatility. *Journal of Finance*, 49:923–950, 1994.

G. Mitra and L. Mitra, editors. *The Handbook of News Analytics in Finance*. John Wiley & Sons, 2011.

T. Miyakoshi. Arch versus information-based variances: evidence from the tokyo stock market. *Japan and the World Economy*, 14:215–231, 2002.

J. I. Myung and D. J. Navarro. *Encyclopedia of Behavioral Statistics*, volume 2, chapter Information matrix, pages 923–924. Chichester, UK: Wiley, 2005.

M. Najand and K. Yung. A garch examination of the relationship between volume and variability in futures markets. *The Journal of Futures Markets*, 11:613–621, 1991.

J. Nakajima and Y. Omori. Leverage, heavy-tails and correlated jumps in stochastic volatility models. *Computational Statistics & Data Analysis*, 53(6):2335–2353, April 2009.

D. Nelson. Arch models as diffusion approximations. *Journal of Econometrics*, 45: 97–127, 1990.

D. B. Nelson. Conditional heteroscedasticity in asset returns: a new approach. *Econometrica*, 59:347–370, 1991.

Y. Omori, S. Chib, N. Shephard, and J. Nakajima. Stochastic volatility with leverage: Fast and efficient likelihood inference. *Journal of Econometrics*, 140(2):425–449, October 2007.

V. Ragunathan and A. Peker. Price variability, trading volume and market depth: evidence from the australian futures market. *Applied Financial Economics*, 7: 447–454, 1997.

J. Ravi, G. Skoulakis, and Z. Wang. Generalized method of moments: applications in finance. *Journal of Business and Economic Statistics*, 20(4):470–481, 2002.

P. Samuelson. Proof that properly anticipated prices fluctuate randomly. *Industrial Management Review*, 6:41–49, 1965.

G. W. Schwert. Stock volatility and the crash of '87. *Review of Financial Studies*, 3 (1):77–102, 1990.

E. Sentana. Quadratic arch models. *Review of Economic Studies*, 62:639–661, 1995.

J. L. Sharma, M. Mougoue, and R. Kamath. Heteroscedasticity in stock market indicator return data: volume versus garch effects. *Applied Financial Economics*, 6(1):337–342, 1996.

M.K. So, K. Lam, and W. K. Li. A stochastic volatility model with markov switching. *Journal of Business & Economic Statistics*, 16(2):244–53, April 1998.

G.E. Tauchen and M. Pitts. The price variability volume relationship on speculative markets. *Econometrica*, 51:485–505, 1983.

S. Taylor. *Modelling of Financial Time Series*. Chichester-Wiley, 1986.

P. C. Tetlock. Giving content to investor sentiment: The role of media in the stock market. *Journal of Finance*, 62:1139–1168, 2007.

R. S. Tsay. *Analysis of Financial Time Series*. Wiley, second edition edition, 2005.

H. White. A heteroscedasticity-consistent covariance matrix estimator and a direct test for heteroscedasticity. *Econometrica*, 48(4):817–838, 1980.

J. B. Wiggins. Option values under stochastic volatilities. *ournal of Financial Economics*, (19):351–372, 1987.

J. Xiao, R. D. Brooks, and W.-K. Wong. Garch and volume effects in the australian stock markets. *Annals of Financial Economics*, 5:79–105, 2009.

Jun Yu. On leverage in a stochastic volatility model. Econometric Society 2004 Far Eastern Meetings 497, Econometric Society, August 2004.

J. M. Zakoian. Threshold heteroskedastic models. *Journal of Economic Dynamics and Control*, 18:931–955, 1994.